HOW TO
Succeed
IN DIFFERENTIATION

THE FINNISH APPROACH

Anssi Roiha – Jerker Polso

First published 2020
by John Catt Educational Ltd,
15 Riduna Park, Station Road,
Melton, Woodbridge IP12 1QT

Tel: +44 (0) 1394 389850
Fax: +44 (0) 1394 386893
Email: enquiries@johncatt.com
Website: www.johncatt.com

Originally published by PS-kustannus

ISBN: 978 912906 88 8

Set and designed by John Catt Educational Limited

CONTENTS

Part 1
THE BACKGROUND OF FINNISH EDUCATION

Part 2
THE BACKGROUND OF DIFFERENTIATION

Part 3
THE FIVE-DIMENSIONAL MODEL OF DIFFERENTIATION IN PRACTICE

Part 4
DIFFERENTIATION IN DIFFERENT SUBJECTS

Appendices

ABOUT THE AUTHORS

THE AUTHORS

The authors have worked as colleagues at a comprehensive school in Finland.

ANSSI ROIHA (PHD) works as a lecturer at HU University of Applied Sciences Utrecht in the Netherlands where he trains pre-service English teachers. Before his career in tertiary education, Roiha worked many years in primary education. He has worked as a student support specialist at an International Baccalaureate school in the Netherlands and as a special education teacher in Finland. In addition to differentiation, his other research interests are CLIL education and intercultural education.

JERKER POLSO (MED, MBA) is a principal and special education teacher who has worked as a teacher and trainer in all levels of education in Finland. He has mostly worked in primary school as a classroom teacher and a special education needs teacher. Polso has also worked in in-service training for teachers and principals internationally. He is the principal of an international Finnish comprehensive and upper secondary school. Alongside work, he writes his doctoral dissertation in in-service teacher training and education exports.

THE ILLUSTRATOR

MIIKKA PAAJANEN (MED) is a classroom teacher and illustrator from Helsinki, Finland. He has previously illustrated learning materials, such as The Finnish Association on Intellectual and Developmental Disabilities. He currently works in a primary school as a classroom teacher and vice principal.

FOREWORD

Differentiation is an approach to education in which every student's individuality and special needs are taken into account. Differentiation strives to give everyone a chance to learn and to experience success. In a classic cartoon, different animals are tested with the same task of climbing a tree. What comes naturally to one is impossible to another. Learning through reading is easy for most students, but due to learning difficulties or problems in concentration, it can prove difficult and strenuous for others. In order for different kinds of learners to reach the same goal, differentiation is needed. Differentiation helps every student climb the tree of knowledge. In our work as special needs teachers, we have been looking for a book that compiles theories and practical examples of differentiation together into one single book that could be recommended to a teacher struggling to help a student with specific learning needs.

One can see many forms of difference at school following the rise of special needs students and immigration. Nowadays, classrooms worldwide are very heterogeneous and teachers encounter many kinds of students in their work. Teachers are often advised to differentiate in order to resolve this situation, but many teachers feel that they do not have enough resources, knowledge or skills to differentiate their teaching. However, these teachers still must think about how each student can progress in their learning as well as possible.

We believe that differentiated teaching is most effective when it is done systematically. It is never too late or too early to start to learn something new. Teachers can create a practice in their classroom in which different solutions are allowed and normalised. Optimally, differentiated instruction is flexible and includes the idea that you don't have to complete tasks in the exact same way as everyone else. In addition, we want to emphasise that differentiation, much like any teaching, must be done in cooperation with the students and their parents and guardians. When there is any concern, the teacher should always contact them. They have invaluable information about the student that can be used when planning the support the student should receive. The most effective approach is to agree upon the methods of differentiation with the student and their parents and guardians. This way, all parties agree to the support, and parents and guardians can take them into account at home.

This book is written from the Finnish context. Due to the focus on equality and student support, differentiation is very much emphasised in the Finnish education system. Indeed, the Finnish national curriculum obligates all teachers to differentiate their teaching from the get-go. We believe that this has given the Finnish education system an advantage. For example, the curriculum states:

> *The selection of working methods is guided by differentiation of instruction. Differentiation is based on the teacher's knowledge of their pupils' personal needs. It is the pedagogical point of departure for all instruction. It concerns the extent and depth of learning, the rhythm and progress of the work and the pupils' different ways of learning. Differentiation is based on the pupils' needs for and possibilities of planning their own studies, selecting different working methods and progressing at an individual pace. The individual and developmental differences between pupils are also taken into account in the selection of working methods. Differentiation supports the pupils' self-esteem and motivation and promotes a peaceful setting for learning. Differentiation also pre-empts needs for support.* – Finnish National Core Curriculum for Basic Education (hereafter FNCCBE 2014)

Even though the book is written with a Finnish viewpoint, it is, above all, meant to be a practical tool in the everyday work of any teacher. The book is divided into four parts. Part I explains the background of Finnish education and differentiation in the Finnish context. It clarifies where our line of thinking is coming from. Part II investigates the theoretical basis for differentiation and strives to offer new perspectives for the most common challenges of differentiation. In addition, Part II introduces you to the imaginary example students, whose problems are attempted to be solved later in the book. In Part III, differentiation is approached through the five-dimensional model of differentiation, which we have created. In our opinion, this model covers the most central areas of teaching, in which differentiation should be acknowledged. In Part IV, differentiation is exemplified in language and literature, mathematics and foreign languages. We have chosen these subjects because they act as tools when learning other subjects. Language and literature skills are needed in all subjects, mathematics creates a basis for all STEM (science, technology, engineering and mathematics) subjects, and learning a foreign language is increasingly important as it is especially highlighted in later studies. The book progresses cumulatively in regard to differentiation. The presumption is that the reader has an understanding of Part III of the book when reading the chapters of Part IV, since Part III also includes tips for differentiation in these subjects. Although the book is very practical and focuses on teaching, it is based on researched information. The appendices at the end of the book include different practical tools and forms to support differentiation.

For the sake of clarity, we use the terms 'high-achiever' and 'low-achiever' when talking about students. However, we do acknowledge these terms and the division between the two are somewhat problematic and simplistic. By low-achievers, we mean students who have difficulties at school and who would, without appropriate support measures, underachieve for one reason or another. By high-achievers, we refer to students whose academic success is clearly above average. We have seen in our work how far-reaching effects the lack of individual support can have. Even though in this book we mainly focus on supporting the weakest students, we will not disregard the most high-achieving students. The book also serves those who work with immigrant students, as due to linguistic difficulties, they often need strong differentiation in the beginning of their studies.

The idea for this book began to mature slowly during our own studies. The discussions between us authors in the everyday school life gave the project the last nudge it needed. In the book, we have compiled tips about differentiation, based on our own experience and observations. The purpose is to share thoughts and practices so that one should not have to reinvent them again in their work. The practices shown in the book are not invented by us, but we have collected them throughout our years of studying, researching and working in education. The biggest thanks is to our colleagues, the old and the new, as well as to the schools in which we have studied and worked. We would especially like to thank Satu Jokinen, who read the draft of our book and gave precious comments, Jarkko Granqvist, who gave us valuable notes on the chapter about assessment, as well as Marja-Sisko Kautto, who helped us make some practices more specific.

We believe that differentiation should be an integral part of one's teaching philosophy, and ever-present in the background of lesson-planning and teaching in practice. We understand that no teacher can surely acknowledge each student in every moment during a school day. However, with this book, we would like to get differentiation included in the teaching culture. Our hope is that differentiation would be seen as something that applies to all students and that its benefits would replace its challenges in our discourse.

We hope that this book can support teachers in differentiation and help them to succeed in it too!

Anssi Roiha and Jerker Polso

Part 1

THE BACKGROUND OF
FINNISH EDUCATION

Finnish education has a very positive reputation worldwide and it is generally considered as extremely high-quality. Needless to say, as Finnish teachers, we are true believers in the Finnish education system. However, above all, we are educators. The point of this book is not to advocate for Finnish education as such, but to share good practices with educators all around the world. We argue that most of the practices presented in this book can be transferred to and implemented in various school contexts. However, we understand the interest that is targeted towards Finnish education practices. In this chapter, we will explain the Finnish education system in short. We feel that it might be useful for the reader to understand the context in which this book was written and where we as educators are coming from. We will briefly address the cornerstones of Finnish education, such as free education, teachers, equality, student support and assessment.

THE FINNISH REPUTATION

The most prominent reason for the Finnish reputation in education is the exceptionally high achievement in previous PISA studies (Programme for International Student Assessment). Ever since Finland first took part in the studies in 2000, it has topped the rankings. Finland has been the highest performing country in literacy skills in 2000, reading in 2003 and science both in 2003 and 2006. In addition, Finland reached second place in overall performance in mathematics both in 2003 and 2006, reading in 2006 and science in 2009. Other remarkable achievements have included the third highest score in problem-solving in 2003 and reading in 2009, and the fifth highest score in mathematics in 2009. (OECD 2003; 2004; 2007; 2010)

Lately, Finnish education has also been a subject of controversy (Itkonen, Dervin & Talib 2017). Some critics argue that the high results have actually been achieved by earlier education models, or that the Finnish society is so homogeneous that the educational results are not comparable with other countries. There has also been a minor decline in Finnish PISA results, as in 2012 Finland had dropped down to 12th place in mathematics, 6th place in reading and 5th place in science (OECD 2014). In 2015, the PISA study measured science, reading, mathematics and collaborative problem-solving. In those areas, Finland ranked 3rd, 2nd, 7th and 5th respectively (OECD 2018). In general, these are still very satisfactory results, but the previous results outperforming the latest figures has been cause for some concerns amongst Finnish policymakers. Regardless of the critique and minor changes in the rankings, Finnish education remains high-performing in international comparison.

The development of Finnish education can be seen as a unique combination of chance and careful planning. Some critics argue that Finland has not had to struggle with similar challenges in education than the rest of the world, especially during the past few decades. They are partially right as the Finnish education system has had the privilege and opportunity to develop in relative isolation on the outskirts of Europe. Our nation has been rather homogeneous in the past, and our teachers are highly educated and valued by society. On the other hand, the nation has been relatively poor and often caught in the middle of international politics. Although history is partly responsible for the Finnish education success, in this book we want to focus on the present trends in Finnish education and point out the deliberate actions taken to ensure the high quality of education in the future as well.

STRUCTURE OF COMPREHENSIVE EDUCATION IN FINLAND

Currently, Finnish education is considered equal and democratic due to the still existing comprehensive school system, which was launched in 1972 in the northern parts of Finland and taken into practice throughout the country by 1979. At first, there were different syllabi for different ability groups, but they were abolished in 1985. Since then, all children have followed the same curriculum (Sahlberg 2011). Interestingly, the comprehensive school system was vastly criticised at the time and blamed for making people exaggeratedly homogeneous and incapable of independent thinking, which is something that has been proven quite the opposite in light of the past PISA results.

As mentioned above, until recently, Finnish society has been rather homogeneous. Therefore, it can be argued that Finland has not had to struggle with the same challenges many other education systems in the world have during the past few decades, for example with regard to different ethnic groups and a vast number of immigrants. Although this situation has also changed during the recent years in Finland, it is good to keep in mind that the fundamental idea behind the Finnish comprehensive school system has been to achieve equity and equality for all members of society. The homogeneous student body can therefore be seen as the end result of the education system, rather than as the cause of it.

In the Finnish school system, the fundamental responsibility for learning is with the students and their families. Interestingly, school is not compulsory by law. However, learning is. Finnish parents can actually get fined if they do not ensure the teaching and learning of their child. In practice, home-schooling is rather rare, as most students attend public education.

Finns begin grade 1 in the year they turn seven years old. A one-year-long pre-primary education is also compulsory for all children. The first part of the comprehensive school, referred to as primary school, consists of grades 1-6 (approx. ages 7-12) and is followed by the second stage, called lower secondary school, consisting of grades 7-9 (approx. ages 13-15). After comprehensive school, students can choose from two different systems of upper secondary schooling; either an academically oriented general upper secondary school or a more practically oriented vocational institution. Up until 2019, upper secondary education has not been compulsory, although over 90% of people attend it (Kupiainen, Hautamäki & Karjalainen 2009). A unique feature in the Finnish system is the fact that there are no dead-ends. The vocational path can lead a student to higher education studies and even a doctorate, as illustrated in figure 1.

Currently, Finnish compulsory basic education (primary and lower secondary school) ends after grade 9 or when the student turns 17, depending on which comes first. At the time of writing this book (summer 2019), the government has announced plans of making upper secondary education compulsory for all students as well. The academic school year in Finland is 190 working days and is reduced by those public holidays that are placed in the middle of the week. Unlike in many other countries, the school year in Finland is divided into two terms. The school year starts in the first weeks of August and ends at the end of May or early June. The school days for students are short compared to many other countries. An average school day for a first-grade student is four hours. This time spent in school is gradually increased so that the average school day for a lower secondary school student is six to seven hours.

EDUCATION SYSTEM IN FINLAND

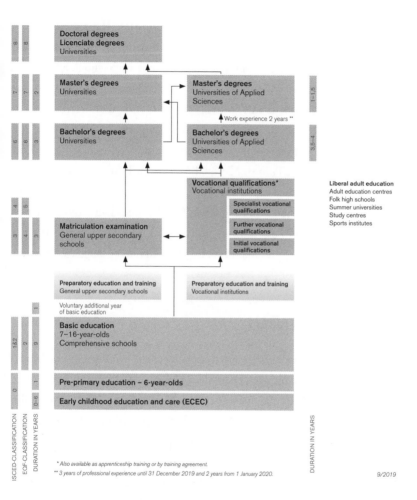

FIGURE 1. The Finnish education system (Ministry of Education and Culture 2019)

A common misconception is that there is no private education in Finland. It is true that the vast majority of Finnish schools are public, and there are very few private schools compared to many other countries. The reasons for this are manifold. Perhaps surprisingly for some, market forces have a role to play in this. According to the principles of the comprehensive school, all children regardless of their socioeconomic background attend the same school. Schools do not select their students and normally students enter their nearby schools. In 2018, there were 560,500 students in Finnish comprehensive schools (OSF 2018a). Only less than 2% of them studied in a private school or in a school that operates under the Finnish National Agency for Education (Perusopetus n.d.). High-quality public education simply diminishes the demand for private education; people do not see a need for it. On the other hand, the legislation and the funding system also favours public schools and education. The few private schools that exist in Finland are usually religious or language-oriented.

FREE EDUCATION FOR ALL

As education is compulsory, it is also free of any charges or tuitions. As the cost of education is covered by taxes, taxation in Finland is relatively high compared to many countries. Studying itself is completely free in basic education. This means that all educational materials, possible transportation and meals are also free for the students. In fact, schools are not allowed to collect any additional charges from the parents. It is worth mentioning that upper secondary and tertiary education are also free, although students usually have to pay for the study materials in upper secondary education, and also for the meals in tertiary education. If, in the future, upper secondary education becomes compulsory for all, the learning materials would also be provided by the schools.

The free school meal is an interesting feature in the Finnish education system, of which the Finns are particularly proud. A free school meal has been a part of the Finnish education system since 1948. As mentioned earlier, all

Finnish students in primary and secondary education get a nutritious lunch from the school. As the quality of the food is good, this option is also vastly utilised. Vegetarian food and different dietary options are also always available. The free school meal ensures equal opportunity for all students regardless of their background and allows them to fully concentrate on their studies while they are at school.

STRIVE FOR EQUITY

All in all, the educational legislators in Finland want to avoid polarisation of education, which is often seen to lead to inequality. As a small nation, Finland cannot afford to leave anyone behind and the best way to avoid this is to ensure equality. The aim is for big variation within a school but a small variation between schools. This is also the reason why ranking systems are not used by the government. The progress of schools is followed by the Finnish National Agency for Education for quality assurance purposes, but the results are not published. The only standardised national test in Finland is the matriculation examination at the end of grade 12. These results are public information and rankings have been done by newspapers, for instance, but not by the government or legislators.

One idiosyncrasy of Finnish education is a very strong culture and tradition of special education and student support. The philosophy behind this is, once again, simple: a child left behind is a taxpayer lost and only leads to costs in the future. Finland uses a three-level model to support the learners. This comprises general, intensified and special support. Out of these, a student can receive only one level of support at a time. Differentiation is emphasised at all the levels and the various different practices that can be employed at each level include, for instance, remedial teaching, the use of school assistants or special aids (FNCCBE 2014). A student's learning is first supported by differentiating before any other steps need to be taken for support (Koivula 2012). Differentiation is particularly used during the first two steps of support, general and intensified support. In special support, the student's instruction and assessment can be completely individual, and due to this, special support is not always connected to differentiated instruction. In reality, we do not believe that the level of support a student gets makes a big difference in the planning and execution of teaching from the point of view of differentiation. No matter the level of support, instruction should progress the same way from the personal goals of the student, through the content of teaching, and to assessment. Thus, differentiated instruction also serves those students who receive special support. Figure 2 elaborates the Finnish three-level model of support.

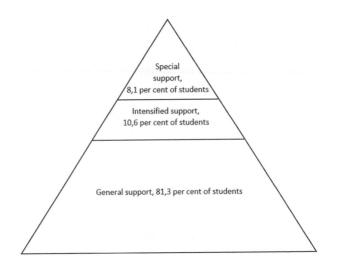

FIGURE 2. The three-tiered support system in Finland

In 2018, nearly one in five students received either intensified or special support. More specifically, 10.6% of comprehensive school students received intensified support and 8.1% received special support. Out of the students having received special support, 35% studied fully in a segregated special group, whereas 21% studied fully in a mainstream education group. The remaining students received their support in both mainstream education and special education groups (OSF 2018b).

The school support services focus on the overall wellbeing of the student. Each school has a student welfare team who guide and follow the students and the school as an organisation. Each school is also assigned with a school psychologist and a counsellor. Additionally, career guidance and counselling are offered as a separate subject from grade 8 onwards. In the early years, it is integrated in all the other subjects. It is worth mentioning that the focus on student support services is paying off, and there are very few school dropouts. Nearly all children in Finland (99.7%) complete comprehensive school (Ministry of Education 2008).

THE FINNISH NATIONAL CURRICULUM FOR BASIC EDUCATION

A few years ago, Finland went through the biggest education reform since the comprehensive school reform in the 1970s. The reform included new objectives, contents and lesson-hour distribution. One central feature of the reform is the new national core curriculum which was first implemented in 2016. The fundamental idea behind the reform was to update the school and teaching to meet the requirements of the world today, and, most importantly, in the future. Although the latest curriculum reform was bigger than usual, the curriculum is and should be constantly revised. The process is renewed every six to ten years, which may lead to the argument that it is constantly revised.

Unlike in some other countries, in Finland the curriculum is written and designed by teachers *for* teachers. The curriculum process always starts from the national level, where hand-picked teachers draft the National Core Curriculum, which then sets the boundaries for regional curriculum work. Each educational provider (municipality) writes their own version of the national core curriculum together with their teachers: 'What are the unique features of our region?' Often this curriculum process is opened even further on school level: 'What does this mean in our school? What makes our school unique? How do we implement the national core curriculum?'

The curriculum work is usually done as part of the everyday workload, although it is often compensated either financially or in the teaching load of an individual teacher. As the process is renewed every six to ten years, each and every teacher who stays in the profession for more than five years will at some point of their career be part of writing the curriculum. This makes all the teachers curriculum experts and deeply involved and aware of the curriculum requirements.

The Finnish national core curriculum starts from values and sets out the content and objectives for teaching. The focus is on transversal competences, which are then taught through individual subjects and content areas. Transversal competence is described in the Finnish national core curriculum as 'an entity consisting of knowledge, skills, values, attitudes and will' (FNCCBE, section 3.3). They are seen as far more important than individual pieces of information. The curriculum lists the following transversal competences:

1. Thinking and learning to learn
2. Cultural competence, interaction and self-expression
3. Taking care of oneself and managing daily life
4. Multiliteracy
5. Information and communication technology competence
6. Working life competence and entrepreneurship
7. Participation, involvement, and building a sustainable future

BALANCED CURRICULUM

The Finnish curriculum is based around skills and competences. The curriculum values all subjects equally. The so-called non-academic subjects are also highly appreciated in the Finnish education system. On top of the academic subjects all students study, physical education, music, hand crafts, visual arts, home economics and guidance counselling are also compulsory subjects. Figure 3 presents the lesson allocation as it is described in the Finnish national core curriculum. The numbers shown in the chart are so-called minimum hours and may vary regionally.

Subjects	Grades	1 2	3 4 5 6	7 8 9	Total
Mother tongue and literature		14	18	10	42
A1-language (First compulsory language)			9	7	16
B1-language (Second compulsory language)			2	4	6
Mathematics		6	15	11	32
Environmental studies		4	10		
Biology and geography				7	
Physics and chemistry				7	
Health education				3	
Environmental and health studies in total			14	17	31
Religion / Ethics		2	5	3	10
History and social studies			5	7	12
Music		2	4	2	8
Visual arts		2	5	2	9
Crafts		4	5	2	11
Physical education		4	9	7	20
Home economics			3		3
Artistic and practical elective subjects			6	5	11
Artistic and practical subjects in total					62
Guidance counselling			2		2
Optional subjects			9		9
Minimum number of lessons					**222**
Optional A2-language (starting in grades 4 to 6)			12		12
Optional B2-language (studied in grades 7 to 9)			4		4

FIGURE 3. Distribution of lesson hours in basic education

FINNISH TEACHERS

One factor behind the success of Finnish education is the teachers. First of all, Finnish teachers are very highly trained. The minimum requirement is a master's degree with education in at least a secondary subject. Teachers are also highly valued and, even today, the teaching profession has remained one of the most wanted amongst university students. Therefore, teacher training universities are able to choose only the top applicants. For example, in 2018 in the university of Helsinki, only 12.6% of the applicants were accepted on to their teacher training course.

Both the schools and the teachers have a high level of independence in Finland. For instance, as opposed to strong standardisation and national testing, the municipalities and schools have had the liberty to decide their specific objectives and contents, as the national curriculum has set the framework for that. Another important feature of Finnish schools is the trust in teachers' professionalism and having no school inspections (Kupiainen *et al.* 2009). Teachers are seen as experts in their field, and they are utilised accordingly, for example, in curriculum work and creating learning materials for teaching.

Teachers are free to choose and utilise whatever learning materials they want. School books and materials are not monitored or pre-approved by any government entity, which makes the development process faster. Learning materials that are available in the markets reflect the needs of the teachers and students well. School books are mostly written by teachers actively working in the field.

TEACHING IN PRACTICE

Teaching and learning in the Finnish education are very child-centred. In early childhood education, there are no formal structured lessons as they are understood in many other education systems. Even compulsory pre-school has no formal subject level lesson-hour distribution. Children learn through play, and the focus is to arouse the children's natural curiosity and will to learn. A more formal lesson structure is introduced during the first years of basic education. First years of basic education focus on teaching learning skills. The spiral structure of the curriculum enables deepening the knowledge and understanding every year. It also helps with differentiation and enables students to learn at their own level.

Finnish school children learn a lot through play and interaction. The curriculum guides and actually forces teachers to use versatile teaching methods that activate students from their desks. The lesson is 60 minutes, but each lesson includes a 15-minute break, which the students usually spent outside playing – regardless of the weather.

One common misconception we often hear is that there is no homework in Finnish schools. This is not true. Finnish students have homework daily. However, the time spent on homework is less than in many other countries. The schools offer some extra-curricular activities, but they are just that, extra-curricular, and although they support the overall learning and growth, they are not that closely linked with teaching and learning and do not affect the student's grades or assessment in any way.

Assessment is the single most powerful tool that guides education. As mentioned earlier, the emphasis in the Finnish curriculum is on skills and competences, rather than on pieces of information. Consequently, standardised testing is not that common, although it is used occasionally. Teachers might use occasional standardised tests to support their assessment, but these tests are neither compulsory nor nationwide. The focus is more on assessment for learning. Assessment is seen both as a tool to measure learning but also as a tool to guide teaching. The Finnish National Agency for Education follows Finnish public schools by occasional testing. These test results are not published, but simply used by the agency for quality insurance purposes. The test schools and classes are selected with random sampling. Not all subjects and grade levels are tested annually. A student may easily go through their entire school career without participating in any other standardised tests than the matriculation examination at the end of Finnish upper secondary school, which is grade 12.

IN CONCLUSION

As described earlier, the Finnish education system has its perks and peculiarities. In this chapter, we have pointed out nine of them:

1. Free education
2. Equality
3. Highly trained teachers
4. Constant reform
5. Focus on student support
6. Learning actively through play
7. Moderate workload for students
8. Learning for life
9. Assessment for learning

At the end of the day, these features are irrelevant unless they reflect directly on classroom practices and the interaction between the teacher and the student. In this book, we try to give examples on how to put these ideals into practice, particularly focusing on equality and student support. The reader might argue that most of the methods presented later in this book are not of Finnish origin, and they are absolutely right. Good quality education knows no nationality and has no home country. It is pointless to argue which came first, the chicken or the egg. It does not really matter. There has been quality education around the world for ages. As an independent nation, Finland is only a century old. The Finnish education system is far from perfect, but it has adopted some of these good practices.

So, what is good quality education and teaching when it comes to differentiation? As an answer, we are not offering you 'the silver bullet'. Instead, we offer you common sense.

Part 2

THE BACKGROUND
OF DIFFERENTIATION

In Chapter 1, we consider how differentiation has been defined and which theories it is based on. We also explain how we understand differentiation in this book, and open up the five-dimensional model of differentiation that forms the basis of the book. At the end of the chapter, we introduce our example students, who will travel with us through the whole book. The book will offer tools for these students' individually differentiated teaching.

Chapter 2 compiles the benefits of differentiation based on research, as well as reasons why every teacher should differentiate their teaching. In that chapter, we also explain how a teacher can easily recognise the need for differentiation. In addition, we go through the most common challenges teachers face with differentiation and offer solutions to them.

1. THE BASIS OF DIFFERENTIATION

Differentiation is a support method for teaching, in which the challenge of difference and individuality is answered, and which is often referred to when speaking of good teaching. However, differentiation is not always defined clearly and its practices are not explored carefully. In practice, differentiation has become an abstract term, which can be understood in many different ways. In the everyday among teachers, differentiation is often found to be a burden, as well as a time-consuming practice, which each teacher does in their own way whenever they have the time and energy to, or whenever they can fit it in. In this chapter, we present some of the most important definitions and concepts of differentiation and describe our point of view about differentiation.

WHAT IS DIFFERENTIATION?

The Finnish National Core Curriculum for Basic Education (the FNCCBE 2014) lifts differentiation up as an integral part of teaching. In practice, there are as many points of view about differentiation as there are people working in the field. Some teachers understand differentiation in a quite constricted and practical way as simply easier work sheets or simplified learning materials. Some teachers view differentiation as a larger whole and think of it as acknowledging the differences between individual students (Berbaum 2009; Mikola 2011; Naukkarinen 2005; Roiha 2014). It's important for teachers to enlighten themselves on the variety of differentiation so that the individual acknowledgement of students can become more common in teaching. The more widely teachers understand differentiation, the more applications they can find for differentiation methods in their teaching.

In literature, one can find some variety in the ways differentiation has been defined. In its broadest, differentiation, or 'differentiated instruction', can be defined as the overall way to approach teaching by acknowledging each student's individuality. With this definition, differentiation can be directed towards different parts of teaching and school life. By this definition, teachers change their teaching in differentiated instruction in order to maximise each student's opportunities to learn (Tomlinson 2014). Sometimes differentiation can be perceived in a more restricted way, where it is only seen to be applicable to certain aspects of teaching and work methods (Lakkala 2008).

In everyday life, differentiation is typically separated into differentiation for low-achievers and high-achievers. Another distinction can be made between integrative and distinguishing differentiation. Integrative differentiation means teaching in which the goal is to get all students to reach the same objectives through differentiation. In distinguishing differentiation the goals for different students are already differentiated based on individual qualities.

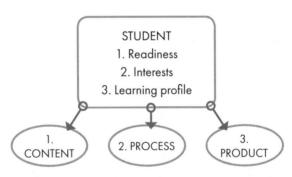

FIGURE 4. Differentiation according to Tomlinson (2014)

One of the most remarkable pioneers and professionals of differentiation is Carol Ann Tomlinson, who has both researched and theorised differentiation

(Tomlinson 2001, 2004, 2005, 2014; Tomlinson & Imbeau 2010; Tomlinson, Brimijoin & Narvaez 2008; Sousa & Tomlinson 2011; Tomlinson *et al.* 2003). Figure 4 demonstrates Tomlinson's idea of the background and execution of differentiation.

According to Tomlinson, differentiation should be grounded in the readiness, interests and the learning profile of each student. She argues that differentiation should be carried out in three dimensions of teaching: the content, the process and the product. By content, Tomlinson means the information and abilities that are being taught and the students are encouraged to learn. By process, Tomlinson refers to the way students learn and can internalise the content being taught. In this case, differentiation of the teaching arrangements and methods is emphasised. The product means differentiating the assessment of learning (Tomlinson 2014).

Differentiation can also be divided into reactive and proactive differentiation. In reactive differentiation, instruction is only differentiated once the challenges emerge. This is possibly the most typical form of differentiation teachers use, and it is very important in principle. However, ideally, differentiation should be proactive, so that it acknowledges the student's individuality from the start. The idea of proactive differentiation is to anticipate the different potential needs of each student, and to plan one's teaching accordingly. Figure 5 displays the model of proactive differentiation.

According to Thousand, Villa and Nevin (2007), proactive differentiation starts from knowing the students. The teacher should get to know their students as well as possible and consider their individual needs, traits and, most importantly, strengths. Proactive differentiation can be seen as a cycle. With the information gained from the students, teachers can differentiate their instruction and observe how the students react, which creates more knowledge about the students and directs the differentiation in the future. In proactive differentiation, constant reflection and monitoring of differentiation are highlighted.

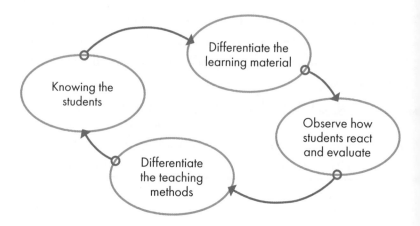

FIGURE 5. The proactive model of differentiation (adapted from Thousand, Villa & Nevin 2007 and Pulkkinen & Rytivaara 2010)

WHAT IS DIFFERENTIATION BASED ON?

Differentiation is not a theory in itself, but includes aspects from multiple theories and concepts. Next, we will present the most important theoretical bases for differentiation. They are grounded in the aforementioned roots of differentiation, which is knowing the student, as well as the student's readiness, interests and learning profiles.

CONSTRUCTIVISM. The constructivist understanding of learning can be seen behind the idea of differentiation. According to the constructivist notion of learning, the action and motivation of the student are vital in the learning process. A lot of importance is also given to the student's prior knowledge and earlier beliefs (Tynjälä 1999; Rauste-von Wright, von Wright & Soini 2003). The student's own interests and previous knowledge are important starting points for the basic idea of differentiation, which makes differentiation a way to apply the constructivist understanding of learning in practice.

THE ZONE OF PROXIMAL DEVELOPMENT. The concept of the zone of proximal development relates to Vygotsky's (1978) socio-cultural theory. Vygotsky uses the concept to refer to the distance between the student's actual development level and their potential development level. The actual development level is the level at which the student is currently. The potential development level refers to the level the student can reach with the help of the teacher's scaffolding. The student cannot independently solve the problems within their zone of proximal development, but needs the teacher's support in the process. According to Vygotsky, the zone of proximal development is unique to each child and independent of the individual's age (Vygotsky 1978). In differentiation, the teacher should be aware of each student's zone of proximal development in order to offer them individual challenges. Because of this, knowing one's students is vital in differentiation. In an ideal situation, each student would work on tasks and activities that correspond to their individual zone of proximal development.

MOTIVATION. In differentiation, the student's interest in the subject that is being learned is highlighted. Thus, student motivation is an integral part of differentiation. For example, motivation lies behind why an individual decides to attempt a task, for how long they want to keep trying, and how much work they are willing to put into completing the task (Dörnyei & Ushioda 2013). In differentiated instruction, the teacher should approach teaching from the point of view of the students' interests, as it increases student involvement and commitment to the learning process. Learning something that one is interested in also has a positive effect on the students' feelings of capability. Thus, the students are better prepared to face more challenging learning situations (Nakamura & Csikszentmihalyi 2009).

THE THEORY OF MULTIPLE INTELLIGENCES. In addition, differentiation reflects Gardner's (2008) theory of multiple intelligences, which he originally developed in the 1980s. In his original theory, Gardner distinguished seven different forms of intelligence: musical intelligence, bodily-kinaesthetic intelligence, logical-mathematical intelligence, linguistic intelligence, spatial intelligence, interpersonal intelligence and intrapersonal intelligence. Since then, he has updated his theory and added new forms of intelligence, which are naturalistic intelligence and existential intelligence. According to Gardner, each person exhibits parts of all of these forms of intelligence, but the levels of each form vary from person to person. He believes that, in teaching, one should better acknowledge different forms of intelligence, because traditional one-sided school teaching has focused on favouring only the linguistically and logical mathematically-orientated students (Gardner 2008). Gardner's theory has been widely criticised for the lack of empirical studies and the use of the term 'intelligence'. However, from the point of view of differentiation, the theory importantly highlights the differences between student learning profiles, which should be taken into account in teaching. Differentiation can be seen as a pedagogical application of Gardner's theory, since the idea of differentiation includes acknowledging each student's individuality.

DIFFERENTIATION IN THIS BOOK

In this book, we draw on the broad definition of differentiation (Tomlinson 2014). By differentiation, we mean an approach to teaching in which each student's individuality and special needs are considered. All practices and principles of teaching, through which the teacher takes every student's individual traits into consideration in order to support their learning and school life in the best possible way, are included in differentiation.

Differentiation is applicable to both low and high-achieving students. However, in practice, due to the lack of resources, one must make value judgements that are reflected in teaching. Most teachers see teaching certain basic concepts to each student one of the most important tasks of the school, and view differentiation for low-achievers more important than differentiating for high-achievers (Roiha 2014). Differentiation for low-achievers perplexes many teachers, and they spend more time in their teaching focusing on low-achieving than high-achieving students (Seppälä & Kautto-Knape 2009). In our work as special needs teachers, we have specialised specifically in supporting those students who are low-achieving and have learning difficulties. Thus, in this book, we will focus mainly on differentiation from the low-achievers' perspective, but we will not forget about the high-achievers and the support they need. Many practices shown in this book can be applied to differentiating instruction for both low and high-achievers.

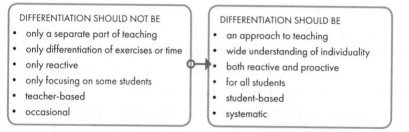

FIGURE 6. The ideal situation of differentiation

We believe that differentiation should be understood as a planned, goal-focused and proactive process, the basis of which are the student's characteristics and the teacher's knowledge of the student. In figure 6, we have compiled our understanding of differentiation.

THE FIVE-DIMENSIONAL MODEL OF DIFFERENTIATION

In this book, we approach differentiation through the five-dimensional model of differentiation – our own creation (see figure 7). The model is not scientific, but a purely practical tool for starting differentiation in a classroom. We believe that, in functional differentiation, the individual needs of the student should be considered in five dimensions, which are:

1. Teaching arrangements
2. Learning environment
3. Teaching methods
4. Support materials
5. Assessment

In one's own work, differentiation can be approached through a single area to make the beginning easier. However, that will not yield the best result. Instead, to fully consider each learner's individuality, one should differentiate one's teaching in all the aforementioned dimensions.

The responsibility of differentiation lies with the whole school community and the individual needs of the student should be considered comprehensively. The five-dimensional (5D) model we introduce includes procedures from general to specific. It is good to start from the broadly general procedures and differentiate teaching arrangements and the learning environment first. Then, one can move onto differentiating with specific practices and tools. In the 5D model, the assessment of learning has an important role. Only when support is sufficiently given in all other areas, can the learning and abilities of a student be assessed in many ways according to the student's needs. Assessment plays a part in helping the students set new goals for themselves. Assessment should be carried out in many different ways, and it should be differentiated and focused on the all-round objectives of teaching. Assessment cannot remain separate from differentiation, but should depict and measure the progress a student makes in reference to their own individual goals. Thus, assessment directs teaching and helps to differentiate instruction.

In the 5D model of differentiation, the student and their characteristics are always the bases for each area. These characteristics include the *learning profile, self-confidence, interests, readiness, needs, motivation, personality* and *personal history*. In this book, the learning profile is defined broadly, and we see it to include the student's skills and the ways of learning that the student finds most natural and satisfying.

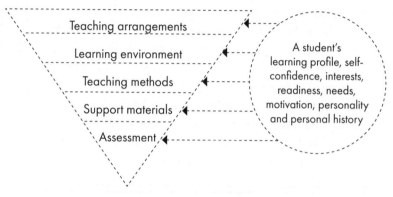

FIGURE 7. The 5D model of differentiation

FROM THEORY INTO PRACTICE. For this book, we have created students for whom school is difficult at present and who would benefit from differentiated instruction. The problems in their schooling are explored in the chapters in Parts III and IV of the book. In the beginning of each chapter, each pupil's individual challenges are described and we will offer solutions through differentiation. For each student, the most useful differentiation tips are compiled at the end of each chapter. In addition, the most applicable modes of differentiation have been listed amongst the main body of the text.

SAM

Sam is a boy in grade 1 who studies in a class of 23 students. Starting school has been difficult for Sam. During the autumn semester, he has exhibited great difficulties in attention and hyperactivity and focusing on schoolwork is difficult. Sam is very restless and finds it hard to sit down quietly on his seat. During the lesson, Sam might crawl around the room and under the desks. Listening to instructions is challenging for Sam. He needs constant instructions to take out his books and equipment. It is also hard for Sam to wait for his turn and to let others work in peace. He impulsively shouts out answers and talks with his classmates during teaching. Sam cannot follow teaching and take part in learning in the same way the rest of the class can. His homework is often left undone. Sam exhibits some negativity towards school and he often says he is tired.

RASMUS

Rasmus is in grade 3 and has a lot of difficulty controlling his impulses and the way he behaves. During breaks and on the way to school, Rasmus is often involved in fights. He finds it hard to correctly interpret social situations and reacts to conflicts with his fists. During class, Rasmus challenges the teacher verbally. He finds obeying unfamiliar adults particularly difficult. Physical education is one of Rasmus' favourite subjects but conflicts and violence are more common during those lessons. Generally, informal learning situations, such as station work or working in groups, are challenging for Rasmus. He really dislikes handwritten activities and often refuses to complete those tasks. In grade 3, the class size is exceptionally large. There are 28 students in Rasmus' class.

AMY

Amy is in grade 5 and has big challenges in school. During the first few years of school she was diagnosed with dyslexia, which makes it hard to learn languages, as well as mathematics. The class groups were mixed before this year and in her new class there have been some instances of bullying. There are 25 students in Amy's class. Amy is quiet and timid in class, but still has some friends at school. Generally, her learning results have been weak. In class, Amy is often left behind and needs constant cheering on from the teacher. Amy is often on a different page than others, but does not seem to even notice it herself. During class, Amy works, but often completely opposite to instruction.

CATHERINE

Catherine is a grade 9 student who is very gifted at school. She is socially intelligent and she has many friends. There are 26 students in her class. Catherine gets bored easily because she completes the given tasks quickly and school does not provide her with sufficient challenges to keep her occupied. Very often Catherine brings a book to school, which she reads after completing her work, while others are still working. During class, Catherine also draws or daydreams. She finds school boring. Schoolwork does not motivate her anymore and she does not see the point in doing her homework. Because of this, lately, some of her homework has been left incomplete.

2. DIFFERENTIATION IN TEACHING

THE BENEFITS OF DIFFERENTIATION

Differentiation has many positive effects on students and, on the whole, the class. This is also supported by research. Next, we will introduce what we believe are the seven most important reasons to differentiate teaching. These are compiled in figure 8.

PREVENTING LEARNING DIFFICULTIES. Differentiation prevents learning difficulties. From a social point of view, learning difficulties only emerge in certain environments. Thus, by moulding the environment, one can affect the emergence of learning difficulties and the disadvantages they bring rise to (Goodley 2001; Oliver 1996). Using differentiation, the learning environment and other aspects of school life can be modified so that certain student characteristics will not be a hindrance to successful learning. For example, using peer support and remedial education, as well as giving systematic feedback, have been shown to reduce learning difficulties in mathematics (Baker, Gersten & Lee 2002; Fuchs *et al.* 2005). It is extremely important to intervene when it comes to learning difficulties since they have been shown to weaken one's self-confidence, which can have a far-reaching effect, even in one's adulthood (McNamara, Willoughby & Chalmers 2005; McNulty 2003). For example, for a student dealing with attention deficits, a restless environment with a lack of structure can cause great challenges at school, regardless of the abilities and skills of the student.

IMPROVEMENT OF LEARNING RESULTS. Differentiation has been shown to improve students' learning results. For example, using flexible grouping and individual tasks has improved the results for both low and high-achieving students (DeBaryshe, Gorecki & Mishima-Young 2009; Reis, McCoach, Little, Muller & Kaniskan 2011; Koeze 2007; Shaunessy-Dedrick, Evans, Ferron & Lindo 2015). In addition, students have been shown to do better in standardised testing when they have received differentiated instruction suitable to their level, even if the tests do not correspond to this level (Grikorenko, Jarvin & Sternberg 2002).

FEELING MORE COMFORTABLE AT SCHOOL. Differentiation can have an impact on how comfortable students feel at school. Students feel more comfortable and are more committed to their work when the tasks and methods are best suited for them. All students do not find the same teaching methods meaningful. Low-achieving students may feel hopeless and high-achievers can feel frustrated if the tasks and challenges are not differentiated so that everyone gets activities to match their level (Sideridis 2003; Keltikangas-Järvinen 2006; Kanevsky & Keighley 2003).

CONSIDERATION FOR INDIVIDUALITY. Differentiation makes it possible for the teacher to interact with their students as individuals. Classrooms can be very heterogeneous. Some people's special needs may be related to the readiness or learning profile of the student. For others, special attention needs to be paid to behaviour and emotional issues. Teachers must differentiate their teaching in order to better acknowledge everyone's individual characteristics that have an effect on their learning or schooling in general (Fischer & Rose 2001; McTighe & Brown 2005; Subban 2006).

EXPERIENCES OF SUCCESS. Differentiation gives everyone the opportunity to succeed. One of the vital tasks of school is to give the student a positive perspective of themselves as a learner. For the lowest achieving students, general teaching can be too challenging sometimes, and they face many failures. This can have a dire and far-reaching effect on the development, self-image and life trajectory of the student (Frønes 2016; Gauffin, Vinnerljung, Fridell, Hesse & Hjern 2013). By differentiating instruction, the teacher can offer everyone important experiences of being successful, which supports the holistic development of the students.

MAKING TEACHING MEANINGFUL. Differentiated instruction has been shown to make school more meaningful for students (Karadag & Yasar 2010; McCrea, Simpkins, Mastropieri & Scruggs 2009). When students work on things they find meaningful, there is a positive effect on learning. Then, students also feel that their opinion matters, and that they have the opportunity to affect their own studies.

IMPROVEMENT IN WORKING ATMOSPHERE. Using differentiated instruction, the atmosphere in the classroom is easier to control. Very often, behind disruptive behaviour there are learning difficulties and instruction that is too difficult (Miles & Stipek 2006; Trzesniewski, Moffit, Caspi, Taylor & Maughan 2006). When they receive work that matches their level of capability, the students have an easier time concentrating and not disturbing the teaching. According to the principles of differentiation, instruction that is linked to the interests of the students makes them more committed to studying, leading to the reduction of disturbing behaviour.

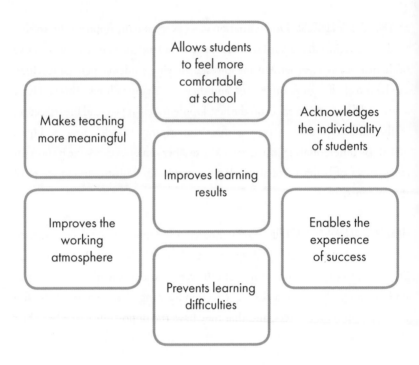

FIGURE 8. The benefits of differentiation

DISCOVERING THE NEED FOR DIFFERENTIATION

Teachers are often unsure about when and whose instruction should be differentiated. The main principle for the need for differentiation is very simple; if a student consistently under or over-achieves at school, one should consider the need for differentiation. The same goes for work habits and behaviour in class. When the practices used in teaching are not working satisfactorily, it is necessary to try something different. As professional educators, we can trust our own observations and act according to them. Monitoring the need for differentiation should be constant. It is good to challenge the students according to their level and not let them off too easy.

Differentiated instruction is often seen as time-consuming. Because of this, teaching is often only differentiated using prescribed learning materials, often a workbook. Designing and preparing individualised learning materials takes a lot of time. This issue is emphasised when there are multiple students in need of differentiation. Instead of pondering about starting differentiation with only one student, differentiation should be made the starting point of all instruction. It is easy to change an activity that is already meant to be differentiated to match the level of all students, even in the middle of a lesson, if the teacher realises that a student is not able to complete the task according to instructions. In later chapters, we will provide practical tips for this.

Differentiation as the basis of lesson planning does not mean that all activities should be widely differentiated. Different kinds of tasks help the student and teacher monitor the progress in learning. In addition, some students are prone to underachieving and completing work the easiest way possible. It is important to keep different levels in mind in differentiation. When the teachers adopt differentiation as a part of their philosophy, they approach all teaching through understanding the students' individuality. Thus, small-scale differentiation, such as individual instruction or homework, is always in the teacher's mind, and this practice becomes automatic depending on each situation. Wide and systematic differentiation solutions, such as added support by a learning assistant or remedial education, should be discussed together with the student and their parents. The decision to move onto big differentiation practices can seem intimidating, and sometimes one needs consolidation for that.

The prerequisite for successful differentiation is knowing one's students well. This is highlighted especially in a new class or when a new student joins the group. At first, it is good to get to know the student as well as possible and in many different ways, such as their hobbies and interests, their pet peeves, and the thing they are most passionate about. It is vital to listen to the students themselves. With the student, one can first engage in informal conversations, in which the student can tell about their preferred learning styles, learning activities, and their school life in general. Very often, the student is pleased to get attention and the feeling that the teacher really is interested in their life. In addition to this, it is good to have a tight connection with the parents of the students, and even meet them at school, as they have valuable information about the student that the teacher should take into account.

As professionals, teachers should also trust not only their own observations, but also the professionalism of their colleagues. We want to encourage professional dialogue between colleagues. There is a lot of information about students at school, and each teacher makes observations about students while teaching. At the very least, conversation with a colleague can open new points of view about one's own teaching, and it can give important information about a student one can use in teaching. Sometimes, there is hesitation at schools about discussing matters related to students due to privacy laws and regulations. However, we feel it is important to talk about relevant pedagogical matters among teachers. Many topics can be discussed on a general level even without naming the child in question. One can also ask other teachers how the student manages in different situations and which practices have been useful in other subjects. Especially a new teacher should talk with the old teacher of the class before the start of the year if possible to discuss pedagogical practices that help the student, as well as challenges the student might encounter.

In everyday life, it is sometimes forgotten that the student has already walked on the path of education for a long time. Even in grade 1, the student has already been instructed by many different professionals. At the very least, one should carefully examine any pedagogical paperwork there exists about the student when one becomes worried about the need of potential support. What documents have been written and what has been written in them? What kinds of observations have been made about the student previously? What kinds of practices have been found to be helpful in learning?

Pedagogical documents are filled in for the student, the home and the teacher, but also to support the work of colleagues. Practical aids to support a student's learning should be actively written down. Documents are meant to support instruction, so they can, and should, be updated even during the school year. If pedagogical documents are not up-to-date, they will not be of much use in teaching. Sometimes, one can update simply by adding an observation and a date. However, it is important to remember active correspondence with the home and cooperation with colleagues when updating pedagogical documents. In addition to this, important information about the student can be found from old tests, different assessments or self-evaluations.

All things related to teaching are not always pedagogical, and this is why teachers should separate student welfare and pedagogical issues, bearing in mind that very often these two do walk hand-in-hand. If you have doubts or questions concerning your students, it is always a good idea to consult the other professional in the school. This could be the principal, school counsellor, school nurse or a colleague.

If conversations with colleagues and pedagogical documents are not helpful for starting differentiation, one can be in touch with the home. As an appendix, we have added a short document that can be used to get a quick overview of the situation regarding the student. It would be useful to have other teachers teaching the student to fill one in too. It can also be taken home for parents to fill it in with the student, or older students can fill it in independently.

In practice, we have noticed that, for example, immigrant families can have a very critical approach to differentiating material and instruction. The questionnaire helps families to notice the needs and challenges of the student. Using the questionnaire as a basis for conversation, it is easier to see that uniform teaching does not always support the learning of the student in the best possible way. We would like to remind that constant assessment and reflection are highlighted in differentiation. This way, one can bravely try different solutions and change differentiation practices to best suit each student, for example through the use of observation and feedback.

Pedagogical documents as support for differentiation

1. Keep documents up-to-date
   - All relevant information related to teaching the student should be in the most recent document.
   - Transfer only the information that is relevant to teaching. Do not copy everything.
   - If there is any information that is irrelevant or unimportant, cut it out.
   - Think about what would help you as a new teacher if you did not know the student and only had to teach them based on the pedagogical document.

2. Remember legibility
   - Write things down in a pedagogical document so that they serve their purpose. Sometimes short bullet points help more than a long description.
   - Write so that the document is accessible to not only your colleagues, but also the students' parents and guardians. Do not use unnecessary professional jargon.

3. The pedagogical document is a tool
   - Pedagogical documents are not only meant for administration, but they are meant also to support teaching. List clear tips and practices that can help with the learning process of the student.
   - Remember to update the document and return to it if necessary. All changes do not have to be made in a meeting with others. Sometimes it is enough to simply mark the date and add a little note (see Appendix 3). The most important thing is that the student and parents have been heard and that they are aware of the updates in the document. Just a message or phone call can be enough.

THE CHALLENGES OF DIFFERENTIATION AND HOW TO ANSWER THEM

Often, teachers find differentiation to be difficult, and many things at school hinder putting it into practice. The challenges that are mentioned most often are the lack of time and resources, dysfunctional physical space, large group sizes, learning materials, lack of knowledge of differentiating methods and a very heterogeneous class (Berbaum 2009; Mikola 2011; Naukkarinen 2005; Roiha 2014; Tomlinson & Imbeau 2010). In addition, some teachers see differentiation to reduce teaching, and think of it as having a negative effect on learning (Mikola 2011; Tomlinson & Imbeau 2010). These challenges surely have an effect on practising differentiation, but it is also possible to alleviate or overcome the obstacles. In this sub-chapter, we seek to offer new points of view about the most common challenges of differentiation. Later in the book, we will show detailed models for differentiating in practice.

THERE IS NOT ENOUGH TIME FOR DIFFERENTIATION

Limited time is potentially the most common obstacle teachers see regarding differentiation. In Finland, SanomaPro conducted a wide-ranging questionnaire in 2014, according to which 71% of teachers felt very busy in their job, and stated that one of the most integral reasons for this was the time taken to differentiate instruction. However, 57% of teachers would like to spend more time for consideration of different students (Toivonen 2014). Differentiation should be approached with small steps. In one's own teaching, one can first think about only a few subjects or areas of teaching, and focus primarily on differentiation there. By only differentiating the learning environment, one can have a considerable effect on some students' schoolwork.

All teaching should be based on the individual needs of the students. However, differentiation should not add to teachers' workloads. Each teacher should think whether or not they have gotten stuck with certain habits that they could re-evaluate. Sometimes in everyday work life, one can forget that a workbook is not a curriculum. Very often, the readily available material from publishers is very comprehensive, and gives opportunities for differentiating for high-achievers. However, with low-achieving students, it is not even necessary to go through all this material. Before rushing on with the book with the whole group, one should make sure that there is a strong basis for learning something new. Sometimes it is good to think whether there is something in your work that you could cut out or give less attention to on occasion. Following and checking on certain learning contents can be done seasonally. When grading essays, one can sometimes focus on whole sentences, and on other times foscus on comma rules. It is also a value judgement, how much time one spends on arduous projects. One should think what will serve one's own students and teaching best.

Often, teachers see differentiation as mainly individualised materials, and find making those to be too much work. However, differentiation can also be done with common materials with the whole group, which is then completed by each according to their own ability. This kind of differentiation does not cause extra work for the teacher. Overall, it makes it easier to combat time constraints if differentiation is present in all planning and execution of teaching. Even including certain principles of teaching in one's own instruction, or using certain teaching methods, serves differentiation and does not overwork the teacher. These practices will be explored further in Chapter 5.

Tips for finding the time for differentiation

- Cut something else out from your work, if possible.
- Start from only one of the areas of differentiation (see the 5D model).
- Make sure you have a good grasp of the basics. A good basis makes teaching new things easier.
- Use the same material with all students, but differentiate in the goals and execution.
- Use teaching methods that can be applied to differentiation.

THERE IS NOT ENOUGH ROOM IN THE CLASSROOM FOR DIFFERENTIATION

Spaces that are too small or otherwise unsuitable can often be seen as a challenge for differentiation. In each classroom, there should be a separate area for group work. For example, it can be a table in the back of the classroom. If that's not possible, this area could be a permanent seating arrangement for some students. Often teacher's desks take a lot of space in the classroom. It is good to think whether the teacher needs a work space in the classroom during class, or whether it could also be used for differentiation. When differentiating, one can also use space outside the classroom. Students who can work independently can sometimes work in the hallway or other spaces at school.

Arranging the desks can affect the way space is used in the classroom. However, according to the principles of differentiation, the learning environment should start from each student's skills and abilities. Each student does not necessarily need to have a desk with their name on it, but instead, one can create a culture in which some students change their workplace depending on the situation. One also does not need to sit by a desk for the entire school day, but they can sometimes be pushed to the walls or form different kinds of workstations in different areas of the classroom, which makes room for differentiation.

A solution to the space problem can be the use of flexible grouping and co-teaching. Students can be divided into different groups between multiple classes and make use of multiple classrooms at once. Differentiation practices like this will be explored more in Chapters 3 and 4.

> **Tips for finding the physical space for differentiation**
>
> - Arrange the classroom according to the situation.
> - Remove permanent working stations, if possible.
> - Move the teacher's workstation away from the classroom
> - Utilise other spaces at school.
> - Use flexible grouping.
> - Practice co-teaching.

THERE ARE TOO MANY STUDENTS IN THE CLASS FOR DIFFERENTIATION

Differentiated instruction cannot be a means to save money, and it should not be used by the administration as a reason to increase group sizes. We strongly believe that teachers in charge of larger groups should have the use of a learning assistant resource, so that differentiation can be easier in practice. On the other hand, large group sizes are also not an impossible obstacle for differentiation. The challenge of large group sizes for differentiation reflects the view according to which differentiation mostly means individualised teaching for every student. In practice, this is never completely possible, or even necessary.

Differentiation can be approached on a group level, so that certain practices and teaching methods can be used to better consider each student's individual needs. In teaching, one can favour cooperative work methods, where low-achieving students get peer support from other students. It is good to remember that students can study different things in the same situation. While instructing a weaker peer, the high-achieving student can learn important social skills. Generally, while differentiating in large groups, different kinds of projects are highlighted. These methods are explored further in Chapter 5.

Using flexible grouping is another solution for differentiating in large groups. Students can be temporarily grouped according to skill level, personality, learning style or area of interest, to name but a few examples. The teacher can focus on guiding one group in more detail, while other groups work more mechanically. A teacher becoming frustrated by a large class size should focus mainly on differentiating the instruction for those students who need most support. However, each student should have the opportunity to study and learn according to their own level.

Co-teaching and cooperation between the school and the home makes differentiation easier. In some subjects, one can occasionally group students based on different criteria in cooperation with the teacher or teachers from neighbouring classes. By doing so, one can target each group with the instruction given to them. Together, co-teaching and flexible grouping also make it easier to target the special education and learning assistance resources towards those who need it the most. Teachers can support the lowest achieving and most challenging groups, in which there are students from different classes. Similarly, the resources of learning assistants can be targeted to the group with the appropriate skill level. Most often, parents are also prepared to actively support their child's school life, but they do not always know how to do that. One should give tips, even materials, for parents to use at home in order to, for example, practice foreign languages or mathematics. With large group sizes, different teaching arrangements are highlighted. These are presented in more detail in Chapter 3.

Tips for differentiation with large group sizes

- Focus mainly on differentiation for those who need most support.
- Practice cooperative teaching methods and make use of peer support.
- Group students together flexibly.
- Practice co-teaching.
- Make parents part of differentiation.

THE LEARNING MATERIAL DOES NOT SUPPORT DIFFERENTIATION

Although there is a lot of criticism about overusing textbooks in teaching, the most commonly used activities at school still come from textbooks (Ekonoja 2014). However, according to many teachers, textbooks are too uniform and do not serve purposeful differentiation. In other ways as well, material is seen as a big problem in differentiation.

Even uniform material can be approached from the point of view of differentiated instruction. Basically, students can complete similar tasks with individual goals. In this case, the students can be expected to complete the same task to a variety of depths. For example, some students can only read the summary from a chapter in a history textbook, translate only some of the most important words in sentences in a foreign language, or only use one-word answers in a first language class. Differentiated completion of activities should be rehearsed sensibly and consistently. When one creates a work culture in the classroom that accepts differentiation from the get-go, students will not feel the need to complain about the different assignments. The other half of the class can sometimes complete the activity orally, while others answer in writing. Different assignments teach a culture of differentiated working styles naturally.

It is good to use different channels when getting learning materials. In many subjects, one can use materials from lower or higher grades. For some student, one can give old textbooks or activity books for differentiated instruction in, for example, teaching first language or mathematics.

Cooperation with other teachers helps with the material issue. One should actively share well thought out differentiating materials amongst one's colleagues. For example, one can create a material bank on the school website, in which teachers can share materials for different subjects. As its simplest, a way to share materials can be a set of pigeon holes in the teachers' lounge. However, efficient use of materials takes a good filing system and a culture of conversation amongst colleagues. A low-threshold method to start this could be by sharing materials with teachers of the same grade as yourself, or simply with a close colleague.

A solution to the material challenge is to do group exercises and projects, in which materials are not so central. The role of materials in differentiation is considered in Chapters 5 and 6.

Tips for overcoming the material issue in differentiation
- Get the students used to a culture of differentiation.
- Use materials from different grade levels.
- Differentiate the same materials.
- Share good materials within the school.
- Practice work styles that can be applied to differentiation.

I DO NOT KNOW HOW TO DIFFERENTIATE

Often teachers feel that it is hard to come up with ways to differentiate. We encourage you to cooperate with other teachers and colleagues. When thinking about things together and sharing the students' situations, one can get good tips from one's colleagues to improve teaching. It is also good to share one's own practices that work well. In addition, one can get good practical tips and solutions for differentiation challenges from the special education teachers at school.

At school, one should address differentiation in a wider scale, for example as a part of cooperative planning. Each school can create its own differentiation principles and practices. They should be physically compiled somewhere so that they can be transferred into teaching more easily. Then, it is also easier to assess them, and new teachers will find it easier to start using them. On a school level, administrative support makes differentiation easier. One can try to bring up the importance of differentiation in the work community, so it would become an important value even on the management level. One does not have to change the whole organisation at once. One can start small, by sharing information with one's closest colleague. Great practices have a tendency to spread more widely in the work community.

Lately, there have been professional development opportunities, such as extra training related to differentiation, more readily available. One should get into these trainings with a few colleagues, and spread the contents of the training to others at one's school. Even a pricey seminar can be worth its price when the information gained can be spread within the organisation, and even between schools. In this case, the costs of the training can be shared between units.

In the literature and studies presented in this book, we have looked at differentiation methods used by teachers. These methods can be used as extra tips in your own work.

ALL STUDENTS ARE COMPLETELY DIFFERENT

In many school districts, the heterogeneity of the classrooms has been increased by, for example, closing down special needs schools. Each student is unique, but often, similar challenges in learning manifest similarly in different students. It may be comforting for the teacher that, in these situations, similar arrangements advance the learning of the student. Differentiation, in itself, answers the different needs of each student.

We encourage to start differentiation in a smaller scale, for example in one subject or one area of teaching, and to be merciful towards yourself. Differentiation starts from small things, and at first it is good to start from one's own actions and making small changes in them. One can ask for feedback from another teacher or learning assistant. One can also record one's classes on video so that one can observe how one gives instructions in class, how one begins and ends a class and whether transitions are clear. Sometimes one can notice surprising models in one's work that make it more difficult for students to learn or even encourage unrest in the classroom. When one's own actions are clear and coherent, it is easier to practice differentiation systematically. In parts III and IV of the book, we give practical tips and examples for this.

Tips for getting ideas for differentiation
- Share good practices amongst the work community.
- Ask the special needs teachers for help.
- Actively participate in extra training.
- Share lessons learned and training costs between units.
- Read literature and research about differentiation.

THE CHALLENGES OF DIFFERENTIATION

I'VE GOT THIS!

ALL STUDENTS ARE DIFFER-ENT!

- Adopt differentiation as a basis for all teaching.

I DON'T KNOW HOW TO DIFFERENTI-ATE!

- Share good practices amongst the work community.
- Ask the special needs teachers for help.
- Actively participate in extra training.
- Share lessons learned and training costs between units.
- Read literature and research about differentiation.

THE MATERIAL DOESN'T SUPPORT DIFFERENTIA-TION!

- Get the students used to a culture of differentiation.
- Use materials from different grade levels.
- Differentiate the same materials.
- Share good materials within the school.
- Practice work styles that can be applied to differentiation.

TOO MANY STUDENTS!

- Focus mainly on differentiation for those who need most support.
- Practice cooperative teaching methods and make use of peer support.
- Group students together flexibly.
- Practice co-teaching.
- Make parents part of differentiation.

I CAN'T DO THIS!

NOT ENOUGH ROOM IN THE CLASS-ROOM!

- Arrange the classroom according to the situation.
- Remove permanent working stations, if possible.
- Move the teacher's workstation away from the classroom.
- Utilise other spaces at school.
- Use flexible grouping.
- Practice co-teaching.

... AND HOW TO TACKLE THEM

THERE'S NOT ENOUGH TIME!

- Cut something else out from your work, if possible.
- Start from only one of the areas of differentiation (see the 5D model).
- Make sure you have a good grasp of the basics. A good basis makes teaching new things easier.
- Use the same material with all students, but differentiate in the goals and execution.
- Use teaching methods that can be applied to differentiation.

Part 3

THE FIVE-DIMENSIONAL MODEL OF DIFFERENTIATION IN PRACTICE

In part III of the book, we will address differentiation using the five-dimensional model of differentiation (see Chapter 1). Each chapter will examine one aspect of the model in detail. First, we will consider different arrangements of learning (Chapter 3) and the learning environment (Chapter 4) from the point of view of differentiation. After this, we will discuss differentiation in one's teaching methods (Chapter 5), and present practical support materials to aid differentiation (Chapter 6). In the end of part III, we will focus on the differentiation of assessment (Chapter 7). Alone, we believe, the chapters do not offer a wide enough picture of purposeful differentiation of teaching. Instead, we believe the reader should immerse oneself in part III as a whole in order to get a comprehensive idea of considering students' individuality at school. However, the 5D model of differentiation offers an opportunity to approach differentiated instruction in small parts. In practice, one can master one area at a time. It should be noted that, in different environments, the different aspects of differentiation work are weighted differently, for example because of resources and the needs of the students.

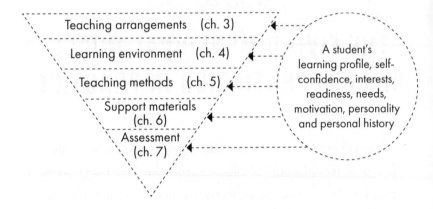

FIGURE 9. Exploration of differentiation in part III, based on the 5D model

3. TEACHING ARRANGEMENTS

The starting point

GRADE 1: SAM

The 23 students and heterogeneous student body make differentiation hard. In Sam's school, there is a strong culture of working alone. Teachers work very independently, apart from occasional co-planning and material exchange. Sam's teacher feels like she does not get enough help with the special needs students and can feel herself burning out.

GRADE 3: RASMUS

Rasmus' class has 28 students, which is a challenge for differentiation and acknowledging each student as an individual. The teacher feels that Rasmus disrupts the lesson often with his behaviour, and by doing so prohibits the whole class from learning. During breaks, Rasmus often gets into fights with other students. Rasmus finds it hard to obey others other than his own teacher, so solving fights will not be successful without him.

GRADE 5: AMY

There are 25 students in Amy's class. The teacher is aware of Amy's learning difficulties and feels bad for having so many students that she does not feel like she can always acknowledge Amy enough. The teacher does not have enough time for remedial education, because she always has other classes or meetings after Amy's school days.

GRADE 9: CATHERINE

In Catherine's school, class sizes are large, even in secondary school. There are 26 students in her class. Some subject teachers only see their students once a week, and are not always aware of all students' individual needs. Teachers feel that they cannot differentiate because of this, so they offer the same instruction for everyone. The teachers at school do not really cooperate, and each teacher is solely responsible for teaching their subject and their own class.

At school, differentiation can be executed through different practical arrangements. Some solutions require structural changes or resources, such as parallel lessons with other classes or assigning classes with learning assistants. However, many solutions can be adopted with very little strain or stress. Often, the lack of money or time is seen as a challenge for differentiation, although one of the biggest obstacles for trying different teaching arrangements is the working culture at a school. Too often, teaching is seen in many schools as an individual practice.

Teaching arrangements that allow for differentiation do not always require more resources and sometimes they can even save you money. We believe that teaching at its best is done in cooperation with a colleague. In many cooperative and differentiated teaching arrangements, teachers have an opportunity to use their areas of strength and interest better than when working alone. For example, it is natural that a teacher interested in coding would use technology to support their teaching, while a teacher specialised in the performing arts would use drama as a tool. The interests and enthusiasm of the adults are often contagious among students. In addition, a motivated and excited teacher will cope and feel better.

It is important to remember that, at first, new methods take more planning than traditional ones. When planning a class together for the first time, the new work method may feel like a burden. However, the amount of work needed will plateau later. When the colleague and new work practices become more familiar, the need for planning together will decrease. In this book, we do not talk about time taken outside of work, but time that has been allocated for teachers to plan their instruction, which can be done alone, but is most fruitful in cooperation with a colleague. If one would like to progress with cooperation and flexible teaching groups in a wider scale at school, one should try to consider time spent together planning even while scheduling classes, for example by paralleling the free morning classes amongst the teachers of the same grade level.

In the first chapter of this part of the book, we will focus on the top dimension of the 5D model, that is, the arrangements of teaching that are most applicable for differentiation. We will go into detail about flexible grouping, co-teaching, paralleling lessons and remedial education. Lastly, we will briefly consider other practical solutions that serve differentiation.

FLEXIBLE GROUPING

On the one hand, large class sizes challenge teachers to differentiate. However, on the other hand, large class sizes make individualised teaching more difficult. This is the situation with Sam, Rasmus, Amy and Catherine. A solution for this is using flexible grouping. Some still see flexible grouping as old, permanent tier groups, in which different content was taught to differently skilled students. In Finland, these tier groups were officially abolished in the 1980s and instead everyone learns the same content that is marked in the national curriculum, unless some subjects are individualised through special support. As opposed to the old tier group thinking, in flexible grouping, the groups are not permanent and do not depend only on the student's skill level or understanding of the content. For example, the basis of flexible grouping can be the students' learning styles, social relationships or areas of interest. It is important that groups are mixed up often and the needs of the students are constantly assessed. Grouping must not be stigmatising and must not negatively affect the student's image of themselves as a learner.

Using flexible grouping, it is easier to differentiate instruction, since this arrangement makes possible, among other things, teaching the groups with specific targets in mind. For example, in a grouping arrangement based on working styles, one group of students can explore a certain topic through drama, another group using computers and another with books. In addition, in flexible grouping, it is often natural to practice cooperative teaching. A benefit of this is utilising peer support. Students often ask for help from one another, and usually support each other's learning quite naturally.

The research results regarding the effectiveness of flexible grouping vary, but there exists some support for flexible grouping being an effective way to differentiate, especially when thinking about all students' learning (Kulik & Kulik 1992; Tieso 2003). From the point of view of learning results, it is important that differentiation is practiced in other ways as well, and not only by grouping students. It is not enough that certain students study together.

The idea of flexible grouping also includes instructing each group in a way that is specialised for them. It is good to keep in mind that sometimes grouping can have a social goal, instead of an academic one. This does not always directly show in learning results. Appropriate grouping makes different kinds of experiences of success possible for students. At its best, grouping can have positive effects on the student's image of themselves as a learner. For example, students like Rasmus practice social skills and group work alongside academic learning. For Amy, working with high-achieving students can be meaningful and strengthen her positive views towards learning, which will then reflect on the learning results.

One can practice flexible grouping either in one's own classroom or more widely, between multiple classes. Students could be divided into three groups, each of which can simultaneously study different things, or the same thing in different ways. Often it works well to have other groups work as independently as possible, while the teacher can focus on instructing a single group at a time. It is good to remember that all groups do not have to work on the same topic, or even the same subject. One group can read independently, and another can do problems from a workbook, while the teacher instructs the third group with mathematics. An appropriate work time for each group could be 15 or 30 minutes, so the arrangement can be executed over one or two lessons.

Flexible grouping between multiple classes makes use of not only teachers' interests and strengths but also the wider school spaces. This arrangement is good to be used first only in one subject, because this way of working can be challenging for the students, as well as the teachers to absorb. At first, the arrangement can focus on very little learned content, with the focus on teaching the new style of working. When planning flexible grouping within a grade level, it is important to consider that students will be populating the groups from each participating class. New situations make most of us nervous, and learning challenges do not make this nervousness easier. Even one familiar face in a group makes one feel more comfortable. However, while grouping, students like Rasmus, who are challenging in their behaviour, can be grouped away from each other or away from those students who spark the negative behaviours.

Flexible grouping can and should be executed across grade levels. For example, a certain science topic could be handled as a project in a group of mixed grade levels. It is good to remember that according to differentiated instruction, students of different ages can work around the same topic with different goals and work assignments. For example, while working on the theme of space, the younger students can familiarise themselves with the planets of the Solar System, while the older students can learn how satellites work. Grouping can also sometimes be done based on skill levels, across grades. In this case, the objective is for each group to work within its zone of proximal development. Students can also make use of and show off their strengths (see Chapter 1: the theory of multiple intelligences, zone of proximal development). When flexible grouping is practiced consistently, different students become more familiar with each other, and working like this becomes easier over time. While working together, students get to know each other within the class, grade level and the whole school. Thus, flexible grouping affects the school atmosphere and community spirit positively.

Flexible grouping applies very well to differentiating for high-achievers, as well as cooperating during transitional phases, such as starting school slowly while transitioning from pre-school to primary education. In this case, the student can move between pre-school and primary school groups based on their skills and needs. A high-achieving student in pre-school can take part in morning mathematics classes in year 1, and a year 1 student who gets tired easily can spend the few last lessons of the day with pre-schoolers. This flexible transitioning needs to be planned-out, agreed on with the parents and written down in a document regarding the student's support. The situation also needs to be agreed on by administration in both pre-schooling and comprehensive schooling, so that every level of education agrees on it and knows their responsibilities in the matter.

If there is a will for it, the administrative obstacles are not overwhelming. In many municipalities in Finland, flexible cooperation in transitional phases is practiced successfully. If needed, pre-school and first grade students can be swapped so that the class size does not change on either side. The most high-achieving pre-school students can show their skills and get to know the world of primary school, whereas those slower in development can make their school work a little lighter. Oftentimes there is also more adult resources in pre-school than in primary education. This arrangement benefits the children and the teachers, as well as the administration.

Some of the teachers in our own school have used flexible grouping successfully. Next, we will present two easily executed ways to practice flexible grouping.

AN EXAMPLE OF FLEXIBLE GROUPING IN THE TRANSITIONAL PHASE BETWEEN PRE-SCHOOL AND PRIMARY EDUCATION

On Thursdays, during 9 to 11am, two lessons have been reserved for primary education to be spent in one's own classroom. This makes flexible grouping possible for the whole primary school. Pre-school students along with their teachers also take part in this. A group from the pre-school nearby is involved in the arrangement, and they visit the school on Thursday mornings. Thus, the average class size has been reduced considerably from normal. When the group is cut in half it is easier to execute the variety of learning practices included in the curriculum.

In the school semester, there are two nine-week terms, and the students from three classes and the pre-school group have been divided into nine groups. The groups have been made in the beginning of the semester, and they have been colour-coded, which makes the groups easier to remember, even for those students who cannot read yet. A lot of time has been spent on making the groups, and they can be amended between the terms.

Teaching is planned together and executed as the same during the nine weeks. During the term, the students rotate with their own group and spend each week's lessons with a different teacher or adult. The teacher leads a lesson with similar content for nine Thursdays in a row, based on their strengths. Thus, the flexible grouping serves not only the students' learning, but also the motivation and energy of the teachers. Between the terms, there is an assessment, and the next term is planned.

Teachers have found working like this very rewarding. It has been thought to diversify teaching and to make planning practical teaching easier. During the nine weeks, one has had the opportunity to improve on the lesson plan one has been responsible for. Teachers have found it especially beneficial for getting to know their students. When multiple teachers teach the same student, there are many adults observing the child. It is easier for the teachers to get information about the pre-schoolers as well, since many of those pre-schoolers would transition to the same primary school the following year. The transition from pre-school to primary education is definitely easier for the little pre-schooler if they already know some of the students and teachers.

AN EXAMPLE OF FLEXIBLE GROUPING IN GRADE 2 SCIENCE

Flexible grouping has been executed systematically among the mainstream and special education classes in grade 2. In this particular school, there are two mainstream education classes and two special education groups per grade level. Thus, in this arrangement, there are four teachers and learning assistants, along with 60 students. Paralleling the lessons to occur at the same time has made this easier in practice.

In the beginning of the term, the students have been divided into four groups. The students have rotated to spend time with the four teachers, each of whom is responsible for teaching a certain topic. They have not used a textbook, and instead the teachers have compiled the materials from different books and sources according to their individual topics. The length of the term has varied based on the learned content.

The groups have been made based on many factors, including skill level or working habits. Group sizes have also varied. For example, the group consisting of students like Sam, who have a lot of trouble concentrating, has been considerably smaller than the others. This group's objectives have been behavioural and working skills, along with the content. For example, two strong special needs students have always been grouped together, so the learning assistant who works with the group has been able to support the participation of both of these students.

Experiences in this arrangement have been positive, both from the teachers' and the students' points of view. This working model has made it possible to instruct the students in a more differentiated and individualised way. The students have also learned many social skills, since they have worked with others, and not only with their own classmates. In addition, many of them have found being taught by different teachers as something that boosts their motivation, as it provides variety. For individual teachers, this method has not been time-consuming, since they have executed the same teaching session for four consecutive weeks. This arrangement has also made cooperation with colleagues a very natural occurrence. In addition, the teachers have learned to know students from other classes better, which has made break time easier, especially when dealing with conflicts.

It is important that differentiation does not stay only within flexible grouping, but that it is practiced also in instruction. For example, in the example about flexible grouping and science classes, the low-achieving students' learning has been differentiated with different work activities. In addition, those students who cannot yet read or write have gotten work that does not require reading or writing. Sometimes the student has done their homework orally and the parent has written it down. Alternatively, the oral homework could also be recorded on the phone. It is good to remember that by differentiating, even a student who cannot read or write can take part in the lesson. The later chapters of this book will give more tips for practical differentiation.

How to get started in flexible grouping

- Practice flexible grouping first in your own classroom.
- Use grouping consistently. Learning a work method takes time for both teachers and students.
- First, only focus on one subject.
- Think about what factors groups are based on, for example work habits or areas of interest, and rearrange the groups periodically.
- Assess the activity consistently and come up with a working model that fits in your own school.
- Ask for the students' input and wishes regarding the arrangements and take them into account.

CO-TEACHING

Co-teaching is an integral part of flexible grouping; a part, which has been used very little, since traditionally, teachers are used to be in charge of and responsible for their own class and planning their own lessons. Past research separates terms co-teaching and shared teaching, but in everyday life, they are used interchangeably. At its strictest, co-teaching can be understood as teaching at the same time in the same space, but in practice, it can also mean shared teaching, in which cooperation and community spirit are highlighted. Co-teaching has a lot to give to resolve the challenges of differentiation. With co-teaching, students' individuality can be better considered at school, and the problem of differentiation in a large group can be alleviated.

Research results regarding the effectiveness of co-teaching vary, but in many studies, it has been shown to be an effective way to support learning (see, for example, Thousand, Villa & Nevin 2006). In Finland, co-teaching has been declared as a positive and practical working model in seven schools in the Helsinki area (Ahtiainen, Beirad, Hautamäki, Hilasvuori & Thuneberg 2011).

The most common way to put co-teaching into practice might be the co-teaching between the class teacher and the special needs teacher. Many schools at least try to arrange the special needs teacher's support push-in, aligned with inclusive thinking. This makes it easier for students who need special support to participate in learning in a larger class. Unfortunately, the special needs teacher resource has gotten smaller in many school districts. Thus, there are not many hours in a week that one class gets to have the special needs teacher there. However, one can practice co-teaching also in cooperation with other class teachers, subject teachers, and, in some exceptional cases, even with learning assistants. In addition, it can sometimes be justified to co-teach with a school counsellor, psychologist, or even with the school nurse. For example, the specialisation of the school counsellor can be used while learning emotional skills, whereas the nurse can help with science lessons. However, we would like to stress that the responsibility for lesson-planning and teaching always lies with the teacher, and those can never be assigned to another faculty member. Nevertheless, it is good to remember that there are many professionals working at the school whose skills and professionalism should be utilised.

At its best, co-teaching is a work method that supports the students' learning and empowers the teacher. The important thing in co-teaching is the shared responsibility, both in planning and in execution. Without planning together and without conversation, co-teaching can be reduced to a role of an assistant or some kind of a behaviour police. Co-teaching requires, not only a lot of time spent together planning, but also wide conversation within the school about the principles of teaching and pedagogy.

There are many different ways to practice co-teaching. For example, Thousand, Villa and Nevin (2006) present four different models for co-teaching, which are supportive teaching, parallel teaching, complementary teaching, and team teaching. It is important to note that the following models are only to point you to a certain direction, and are not mutually exclusive. In practice, co-teaching can have characteristics of all models, and the way co-teaching is used can change depending on the students and the situation.

1. SUPPORTIVE TEACHING

In this model, the other teacher has main responsibility about giving instructions to the class, while the other teacher works among the students to give individual and targeted support. For example, in mathematics class, one teacher can teach something from the front of the class, while the other teacher instructs the same thing in more detail to those who need support.

2. PARALLEL TEACHING

In parallel teaching, both teachers are simultaneously instructing a part of the class in different areas of the classroom. The teachers can be responsible for their group for the whole lesson, or the groups can switch stations halfway through the lesson. In the latter case, the teachers would teach the same thing to both groups. In this model, it is important to focus on the reasons why groups are formed as they are, and pay attention to not grouping the students always in the same way, for example according to their skill levels.

3. COMPLEMENTARY TEACHING

In this model, one of the teachers has main responsibility for teaching the whole class, while the other teacher simultaneously fills in the gaps and makes the teaching more diversified. This model differs from supportive teaching in that the complementary teacher is also addressing the whole class, instead of a few specific students. For example, one teacher can teach something in front of the class, while the other writes down notes on the board for the whole class. Alternatively, the role of the complementary teacher can be to specify or to clarify the instruction of the other teacher.

4. TEAM TEACHING

Team teaching refers to a form of co-teaching in which teachers plan, execute, and assess teaching together. Teachers are both equally responsible for the course of the lesson and the learning of the students. For example, teachers can instruct the whole class one after the other, while the other assumes a more supportive role. In this mode, teachers can smoothly use their specialisation. For example, in a foreign language class, the teacher who has better command of the language can teach grammar, while the other teacher, more specialised in music, can teach an educational song to the group to support the learned topic. The roles of the teachers are equal in team teaching, and the students see both teachers as one another's equivalent.

If the physical spaces in the school cause difficulties in teaching large groups together, the arrangement can sometimes be put into practice by teaching a part of the group in a different area, regardless of co-teaching. In this case, students can be divided into unequal or different-sized groups, which makes more efficient teaching possible. For example, out of two classes of 25 students, one teacher can take 15 at a time to teach them more intensively. Meanwhile, the other teacher can oversee the other 35 students' work. The groups do not always have to study the same thing. In a bigger group, a teacher can lead a sing-along in music, or a team sport in physical education. Thus, co-teaching can save resources and make possible only teaching half a class.

In terms of differentiation, co-teaching gives the opportunity to consider students like Sam, Rasmus, Amy or Catherine individually. Students benefit from the specialties and professional skills of the teachers in this work method. For example, a teacher specialised in cooperative learning can be responsible for instructing this kind of learning method, while another teacher can adopt a supportive or complementary role. Similarly, a musically or visually artistic teacher can take the lead in the artistic subjects. In co-teaching, the teachers' knowledge of the students increases, which will steer differentiation in the future.

IMAGE 1. Co-teaching requires a common understanding of the basics of teaching

It is good to put effort into co-teaching, even from an administrative standpoint. Practical co-teaching can have a great effect on sharing and developing know-how within the work community. All teachers do not have the resources or motivation to take part in courses, which are mostly held outside of work. One could encourage an older, more experienced classroom teacher and a recently-graduated novice to take part in co-teaching. Both of them will learn new working methods and practices from each other. This way, the learned things are practical and certainly applicable to one's work as a teacher. Thus, co-teaching can have a role in professional development. Skills and abilities can be shared within the organisation without even noticing it.

Co-teaching can be made possible by structuring the schedule, but without training the whole organisation, its effectiveness depends on personal chemistry. At its best, co-teaching works like a dream; colleagues complete each other's sentences and understand each other clearly. At its worst, it is a hindrance to a teacher, which becomes a burden and a stressor. Co-teaching can be stressful especially when the teachers have a different approach to the basic principles of teaching, such as planning, discipline or pedagogical philosophies. If the organisation does not yet have a long history of co-teaching, it should be started carefully with a trusted colleague. Each of us has at least one colleague whose skills in group handling or work methods we admire. What if we walked up to them tomorrow, tapped them on the shoulder, and suggested trying co-teaching in some subject or study module?

Things to consider while co-teaching

- Co-teaching can be practiced with a special needs teacher, classroom teacher, subject teacher, learning assistant, or even a psychologist, counsellor or school nurse.
- Try the arrangement first with a teacher with whom you can collaborate.
- Start small. You do not have to do everything together at first.
- Plan the lessons together.
- Spend time discussing basic principles of education.
- Try different kinds of teaching models, for example supportive and complementary teaching, as well as parallel and team teaching.
- Utilise your strengths in executing the lessons.

PARALLEL LESSONS

Paralleling lessons means situating them in the same place in the schedule for two or more teachers. By paralleling lessons in the schedule, co-teaching is made easier and, for example, special needs resources can be allocated better. Along with the budget, the schedule is one of the strongest tools of pedagogical leadership.

Paralleling lessons serves more flexible teaching arrangements. In addition to making flexible grouping easier and saving resources, paralleling lessons brings a new opportunity for flexibility in lessons. Often, only lessons for the whole class are paralleled. However, sometimes it might be cost effective to really focus on flexible grouping and teaching arrangements by assigning two, or even three, teachers for one group.

Part-time special education resources are sometimes still executed completely as individualised or small group teaching. Although this may give good results for individual students, it only serves a very small part of the students at the school. Paralleling lessons among the grade level, for example in foreign languages or mathematics, makes it easier to use special education resources more efficiently. It also makes the everyday life of teachers easier. If teachers also plan their lessons together, the resource of special needs support can be optimally efficient.

Teachers should remember that scheduling often includes compromises. One cannot have everything. Paralleling lessons is easy in classroom teaching, if each teacher teaches their own lessons. In those cases, the only conditions for the schedule are school transportation and teaching spaces. Often, classroom teachers swap lessons amongst themselves or teach some subjects to other classes in addition to their own lessons. Then, it is already considerably harder to find time together. The more classes are taught by different teachers, the more difficult it is to execute a schedule. We encourage open conversation about all teaching possibilities. A motivated, excited and professional teacher can certainly offer diverse teaching and can sustain this throughout the school year. In addition, parallel lessons and the time spent planning together brings more energy into the work, which benefits the students.

If paralleling lessons has not been considered while planning the schedules, one can ask about the situation within the grade level or in the teachers' lounge. Classroom teachers can find common lessons more easily, but for subject teachers, the situation can be more difficult. It is easiest to find out about common lessons from the person in charge of scheduling at school. A teacher who is only beginning to differentiate their teaching should not care too much about paralleling all lessons in the school. We encourage you to start small. With a colleague, find one lesson per week, during which you can try flexible teaching arrangements and co-teaching.

Parallel lessons

- Paralleling lessons makes executing flexible teaching arrangements and methods possible.
- Paralleling also allows for teaching half a group.
- Assigning multiple teachers for one group.
- Paralleling lessons brings the special education needs resource to be used more equally by all students. It saves the resource and makes both co-teaching and small groups possible.
- It is important to also parallel the time spent together planning.

REMEDIAL EDUCATION

One of the integral means of differentiating instruction is giving remedial education. The meaning of remedial education is to prevent and alleviate learning difficulties. Remedial education can be given pro-actively or reactively. With students like Amy, it is often best to get a basis for content that will be taught in class later, if the content could be seen as challenging. This way, low-achieving students have an idea of what will be taught in class, which makes keeping track of the teaching easier. For example, in mathematics, while learning to tell time, the lowest achieving students should be introduced to the topic even prior to the lesson, since telling time is often difficult for those students. For students like Amy, it would be useful to offer remedial education in mathematics, language and literature, and foreign languages.

In group teaching, remedial education can sometimes be used to differentiate for high-achievers. Students like Catherine can take part in remedial education for higher grade levels and make use of the extra teaching time by inquiring into a topic, for example in the form of a project. When upper secondary students go through the Pythagorean theorem, a student like Catherine could join the group.

There are many ways to arrange remedial teaching. It can be arranged for a group of students who need support, or, in exceptional situations, individually for a struggling student. However, individual remedial education is not justified from the perspective of resources. There are certainly multiple students at school who could benefit from teaching the same topic. The person giving remedial education does not have to be the student's own teacher, and it can be given by any teacher at school. For example, in Amy's situation, in which her own teacher does not have time for remedial education, the student could get it from another teacher or a special needs teacher.

It is good to remember that remedial education does not have to last for an entire lesson at a time. Very often, short remedial education sessions are most effective. The teacher can arrange these over breaks, or even before the school day starts. The student can sometimes take part in lessons in a different class at the same grade level, or at a grade lower. This makes it possible to revise topics that the student has already learned. This kind of an arrangement does not take any remedial teaching resources. Sometimes, a high-achieving student like Catherine can take part in lessons on a higher grade level. For example, if a student has prior knowledge and understanding of a foreign language studied at school, it can be justified that they take part in language classes at a higher grade level than their own. Every child should study at their own level when possible.

Options for remedial education

– Offer remedial education for students who need it.
– Keep the remedial education session an appropriate length.
– Practice remedial education pro-actively, if needed.
– Give remedial education to a small group, or, in special circumstances, individually.
– Remedial education can be given by any teacher at school.

OTHER SOLUTIONS

Assistants are an important help in differentiation, and often they have received relevant education for that. We see assistants as aids for the student and their learning, which is why we want to use the term learning assistant. Surprisingly, in many countries, learning assistant are not excessively used, even though they are a cost-efficient and an effective way to support teaching and learning. The learning assistant resource can be used effectively in flexible grouping or co-teaching, as previously mentioned. Unfortunately, learning assistants are often made to work with the lowest achieving and badly behaved students in a different space than the other students. However, the arrangement could, and should, be done in reverse; sometimes the learning assistant could take the highest achieving students to a different place, while the teacher stays in the classroom to instruct the lower achieving students in a more enhanced way. Learning assistants should be educational professionals who have pedagogical experience and from whom one can get good tips for teaching. Usually, it is the learning assistant who sees the students in different learning situations and with different adults most often.

Especially in the lower grade levels in Finland, teachers sometimes have lessons in their schedules, where the group is split in half. These 'split lessons' are lessons during which only half of the students are in class, while the other half has another lesson. These kinds of lessons are very good for differentiated instruction. Often, teachers have set times and subjects for split lessons. However, from the perspective of differentiation, split lessons should not always be spent on one subject, but should be utilised flexibly for different subjects, based on the situation and the needs of the students. Split lessons can also be used in differentiation so that a low-achieving student participates in all split lessons. Thus, the teacher can better differentiate that student's teaching, as the group size is smaller. The split lesson can also work as a remedial education lesson for a low-achieving student when a new or challenging topic is taught in class. This kind of a remedial lesson does not consume school resources. Co-teaching can also be used during split lessons.

Sometimes, the student's situation may call for support actions that are more in-depth than those explored in this chapter. These cases require a multi-professional approach, and thus, the situation is handled in a student welfare group, in cooperation with the parents and the student. Very often, the school psychologist's observations can give the teacher important information about the student's learning profile, which aids in planning the differentiation practices.

Sometimes, the student's situation can be so serious that they cannot stay at school for the whole day. In these cases, it is good to see whether the student could benefit from a temporary shortening of the school day. If attending school is especially burdening for the student, they can temporarily end their day an hour before the others. Sometimes it can only be necessary to shorten Mondays or Fridays, since often the beginning and end of the week are the most straining. These solutions should always be agreed on in good collaboration with the home, so that the student's progress in learning can be safeguarded even though the student studies at home for some lessons. On the other hand, if this solution is agreed on, it is mainly used to support the mental welfare of the student instead of other academic goals.

Sometimes a child is struggling so much that normal school hours are too much. In these situations, temporarily shortening the school day might be the best option for the child. Legislation obviously varies from country to country and usually temporarily shortening a child's school day requires an administrative decision. Regardless of the legislation, it is essential that this decision is made together with the parents. It is also important to remember that shortening the school day should be one of the last support methods, and that the student's day should be lightened and supported by all other possible differentiation methods before this is put into place. In this book, there are many models for lightening the student's day and schoolwork. On the other hand, it is best for the student that the time spent at school is without fights or failures, and that the parents do not have to come pick their child up in the middle of the day. Sometimes, shortening the school day makes this possible. However, this practice should always be a temporary solution, and the situation should be re-evaluated consistently.

Tips to remedy the starting point

GRADE 1: SAM

- Try co-teaching with a good colleague in one subject. Also, offer to help the colleague as well.

- Group students flexibly in your own classroom. Remember that, while differentiating, students can also study different subjects at the same time.

- Consider the possibility of dividing the group in half with two teachers (see co-teaching).

GRADE 3: RASMUS

- Group students at school even across grade level.

- If needed, make the school day or learning objectives lighter. Set goals to ones that are possible to attain.

- In serious situations, consider temporarily shortening the school days. This will be done in cooperation with the parents. Remember to check local legislation.

GRADE 5: AMY

- Give remedial education either pro-actively or reactively.
- Try co-teaching with a colleague.
- Take advantage of the possible resource of a learning assistant.

GRADE 9: CATHERINE

- Offer extra instruction. Utilise remedial education if needed.
- Utilise the learning assistant resource.
- Direct the student to lessons with higher grade levels. Parallel lessons help flexible transitions between groups.

4. LEARNING ENVIRONMENT

The starting point

GRADE 1: SAM

Sam gets distracted by even the smallest of sounds. He spins in his chair and talks constantly. While others work independently, Sam may crawl around under the desk. In Sam's class, there are windows outside on one wall, and on another wall, there are interior windows, showing the corridor. Especially during lunch time, many students walk past along the corridor, since the classroom is very close to the canteen. Moving around in the classroom is hard, because there just is not that much space. The classroom is small, and the desks are almost touching each other. The students' backpacks are strewn on the floor.

GRADE 3: RASMUS

Rasmus' lessons start with at least 15 minutes of solving a fight that happened in the hallways or during break. Altogether, for Rasmus, it is hard to start working. While participating in teaching, Rasmus tends to shout out answers and comments from his seat. There is a bad group atmosphere in Rasmus' class. Wrong answers are sneered at, and bits of eraser are flying in the air. There are often fights during break time, and it takes time from teaching to resolve them, although they are never completely resolved.

GRADE 5: AMY

Amy is mostly quiet and tries not to attract attention. It is easy to blend into the background while others talk. Amy does not put her hand up or ask anything, because she is afraid others will laugh at her. She is constantly on another page and problem than the teacher and other students. Amy's classroom is small. It is hard to find space for students' work or visual materials. All free space is used and crammed full of stuff. A lot of the wall space is covered by cupboards, of which there are still too few, since the classroom is also being used by language teachers. Because of the lack of storage space, even the teacher's desk is overflowing with stuff. The teachers who use the classroom have split the space between them; space is even taken on the whiteboard, as each teacher has a little section for their own notes.

GRADE 9: CATHERINE

During breaks, Catherine is social, but she withdraws during class. Catherine is talented and knows her content, but in class, she does not bring her knowledge forth, since it is not socially acceptable in her group to be academically successful. Often, the air in the classroom is deoxygenated. Because of that, Catherine feels tired in class, which shows as restlessness and disrupting the class.

IMAGE 2. The learning environment can also make school more difficult

The learning environment is often seen to comprise only the physical classroom or an online learning site. However, in reality, it is a much wider concept than this. The psychological and social atmospheres of the classroom, and the school as a whole, strongly affect learning and teaching. In short, the learning environment is everything that encompasses learning and teaching at school. In this chapter, we approach the learning environment first from the physical perspective, and then from the social and psychological points of view.

Physical and psycho-social environments affect each student differently. The workstation or method that works for one student perfectly may be a complete obstacle for another. For one student, listening to music helps them to focus on mathematics, whereas another student may find this too overwhelmingly stimulating. Because of this, differentiating the learning environment can have a great effect on school life. Although differentiation tries to cater to the individual needs of all students, one cannot always change the common learning environment to fit everyone. In practice, the learning environment should be changed according to the needs of the student who needs it the most.

THE PHYSICAL LEARNING ENVIRONMENT

With the physical learning environment, we mean the actual space in which learning happens, and its structure. This includes the school building, the classroom and the tangible objects within them. The basis of changing the physical environment should naturally be the learning of the student, and not the personal preferences or comfort of the teacher. Even in the physical learning environment, the teacher should periodically challenge themselves to wonder about the reasons why they prefer things a certain way. Do I only want desks in the classroom because it has always been like that? What and how do I want to teach? And how do the students learn best?

BEGIN WITH THE BASICS

At first, one should make sure that the conditions in the classroom are optimal for learning. For example, one can often improve learning by controlling the temperature, air quality or lighting of the classroom. If the student is constantly cold, or the air in the classroom is deoxygenated, the issue usually affects the whole class and not only an individual student. When the learning environment as a whole serves the purpose of teaching, it can be differentiated in detail based on the needs of an individual student.

The teacher does not often get to have a say in the shape or size of the teaching space. However, one can make the space better suited for teaching by arranging the seating and other furniture. Does each student see the board? Have adjustable desks and chairs been set to the correct heights? Are technical equipment placed in the classroom in a smart way to allow for teaching? Is the classroom clean and orderly? Is the classroom safe?

Whether one can affect the design of the classroom, the best options for teaching and differentiation are flexibly adjustable or transformable furniture. These can be a shelving unit on wheels, or multiple small tables instead of one large table. Even if one had no say in the architecture or furniture of the classroom, one can often improve a single child's learning by light arrangements. In many new school buildings, so-called aquarium classrooms have become more and more common. Windows outside and into the corridor make the room feel airy, but a car driving past the window or another student in the corridor can distract a student with attention difficulties, like Sam. Curtains, textiles and partitions are cheap and help the student to direct their attention on the necessary. Furthermore, they reduce sounds and put boundaries to the student's field of vision. A neutral colour scheme and low noise level can improve learning, but tending to them usually takes big investments. To help single students focus better, one can use different solutions, such as noise-cancelling headphones or allowing students to listen to music. We will tell you more about these methods in Chapter 6.

ARRANGE, ORGANISE AND LABEL

An optimally differentiating learning environment is organised. In the classroom, all things have their own, permanent, named places, which everyone knows. Behind naming the places, there may be an individual need, but this practice benefits everyone. When things are easy to find, each student can get started on their work promptly. The student knows where the colouring pencils and scissors are, where work sheets and tests are handed in, and where one can go to check one's work. This instruction can be verbal, written, or in picture form, depending on the need and age of the students. The instruction does not need to be limited to the lower grades. With slight adjustment, this can also be done with older students. Labelling the places for different objects can be used to support language acquisition for higher grades. In this case, foreign instruction and supportive material serve language teaching or work to differentiate for high achievers. Picture support helps the lowest achieving students in directing their actions, and the text in a foreign language next to the picture helps others to learn vocabulary.

Labelled places apply to not only equipment, but also to the students themselves. When there are different places in the classroom for quiet reading and group work, physical location and movement direct the student's working. However, the places do not have to be similar for all students. For example, if Rasmus reads best lying on the floor in the back of the classroom, his reading spot might as well be there permanently.

VERBALISE AND OPEN UP THE DIFFERENTIATION PRACTICES FOR THE STUDENTS

Differentiation should not be a punishment or a mark of bad abilities in the classroom. Instead, it should be automatic, and an obvious thing in teaching. However, what is obvious to the teacher might not always be obvious to the students. When our student Sam takes more time to start his individual work and he is moved to a different place in the room, the student and teacher may see this in different ways. From the point of view of the students, the move is a punishment for disrupting the class, even though in reality Sam just needs a quieter working environment in order to get started. Verbalising things to all students helps them to understand and consider different needs. At its best, this increases the self-knowledge of the students, as well as their approval of differences. Thus, this practice improves the learning of the whole class. This method helps the student understand themselves as a learner. When he gets older, Sam will be likely to independently choose a seat that is in a calmer environment when starting his work.

CHANGE WORKSTATIONS AND THE CLASSROOM ACCORDING TO INDIVIDUAL NEEDS

Often, classrooms are similar to each other all over the world. Usually, even the workstations of the students are identical, even though students have different needs and ways to learn. Not counting students who use specialised technical equipment, such as an aid for the blind, there are hardly any differences between students' workstations. One hears common practices be justified by calling it equal treatment for all students, which students pay a lot of attention to as well. It is important to remember that true equity does not mean treating everyone, even children, completely equally, if differing practices can be well-justified. Teacher should not be timid to explain the situation or use different workstations for the students. For a hyperactive student like Sam, an exercise ball or an office chair on wheels could work as the student's chair. Placed in the back of the classroom, these seats allow for small movement without distracting others. Helpful equipment like this are explored more in Chapter 6.

In the classroom, there are often multiple students, whose work and learning should be directed by differentiating the learning environment. It is clear, that not every one of them can sit away from others, near the teacher's desk. However, a single student's workstation can be amended by general arrangement of the classroom, including the use of curtains and partitions, as already mentioned in this chapter. Changes can be made to the classroom even during a lesson. Students can move their desks in no time at all, and get some physical exercise during that as well.

MAKE DIFFERENT WORKING STYLES POSSIBLE IN THE CLASSROOM

In a traditional classroom, students have a workstation for individual work, but seldom have a space for group work. Some innovative classrooms have eliminated desks altogether. The reality that best serves learning is probably somewhere between these extremes. The workstation of a student needs to fit its purpose. One cannot learn to hold a pencil properly while lying down on a sofa.

All students learn and work in different ways. In special needs classrooms, there are often sofas and bean bag chairs, on which students can read and relax. Although money, and especially lack thereof, often affects the arrangements one can make, working cultures are often very different. From the point of view of mainstream education, we might have a hard time understanding that a student lying down on a sofa is actually hard at work. However, first stop to think where you would rather read a book that requires concentration. Would you rather read it sitting on a hard chair, or lounge on a comfortable sofa?

While planning the differentiation of the classroom, if possible, one should attempt to make sure that there would be a purposeful place for different kinds of work; there should be a place for writing and reading, as well as for pair and group work. In reality, this is often challenging. In everyday work life, there is only enough money for the bare essentials, such as the learning materials, and money runs out when whole classrooms should be re-furnished. Even new classrooms can be underestimated compared to the number of students inhabiting the room. It is good to remember that one classroom does not have to fit everything. It is enough that there are different kinds of work spaces within the school. Here, cooperation within the school is highlighted. One should start with a couple of good colleagues, so that teaching spaces can be differentiated between different classes. In this arrangement, one classroom can have seats for individual learning, another for group work, or perhaps reading. Utilising the spaces of the whole school in teaching not only benefits the children's learning and the curriculum but also aids in the everyday problems of the classrooms, such as the quality of air in a classroom which is too small for the number of students in it.

With differentiation, one tries to meet the needs for the students and to create equal opportunities for learning. If there is little money or space, it is good to think how often all students really need to work in the same space, in the same way and at the same time. For a student who needs support, a named, permanent workstation can often be necessary. Clear places and structures create safety and support learning with most primary students. The permanent workstation does not necessarily need to be a desk, and it can be located at a group workstation. All students do not always need to fit around the group workstations at the same time. From the differentiation perspective, the whole classroom does not have to be furnished or changed around all at once. Most students can work independently, but Amy might need a workstation suitable for work in pairs, so that she has peer support readily available.

PICK THE SEATING ARRANGEMENT BASED ON THE NEEDS OF THE STUDENT

With differentiation, it is important to think about each student's individual needs. Often, a student who is easily distracted or disruptive is made to sit in the front of the class, under the watching eye of the teacher. For some students, this can be an excellent place to work in. However, for some, being placed in the front row can make matters even more challenging. From our example students, Sam and Rasmus would more likely benefit from a place in the back of the classroom instead of the front. If the distracted child has the need to constantly see their environment, the seat in the front of the class causes most disruption, as, in order to see what causes each little rustle, the student needs to turn around in their seat each time. From the back of the classroom, the same could be achieved by simply lifting one's gaze up to look at the class. In addition, students like Sam can sometimes get up from their desk to move around, without distracting others.

While planning workstations and the seating arrangement, one should think carefully about the needs of the student and what really disrupts the learning in the classroom. Is it simply the lack of clarity in giving instructions, or is there an attention deficit that could need some more arrangements? The seat that works best can be found by trial and error. When planning the seating arrangement, one should also ask for the students' opinions.

Generally, the students should practice using different seating plans and work methods during primary school, but all students do not have to practice the same thing at the same time. The seating arrangements can and should be differentiated. For Rasmus, even independent work is difficult, so the teacher should not expect him to be able to work in pairs or in a group. Similarly, although most students sit individually, some of them could benefit from sitting near a responsible and attentive student like Catherine, from whom they could sometimes check the correct page number. The different needs and challenges of the students define the appropriate work methods. Although one should practice team work at school, sitting in pairs can disturb a student's concentration on their own work and studying. One can learn to work in pairs during lessons in other ways than only by sitting next to one another.

CHOOSE VISUAL MATERIALS BASED ON THE STUDENTS' NEEDS

Although all students are not distracted by disorganisation, a clean and organised classroom does not make it harder or slower for anyone to learn. From the perspective of differentiation, cleanliness means a sort of simplification, since often one tries to improve the classroom atmosphere by putting up posters and pictures. One means well by doing this, but too much stimulating material on the walls can work against a student with an attention deficit. If there are too many stimulating objects in the room, the student can have a hard time finding the essential information amongst all the nice and colourful things. A beautiful poster can bring one's thoughts away from teaching. For a student like Sam, who has a hard time concentrating and paying attention, this can cause attention to be paid everywhere, and not only where the teacher wants. Especially when there is not a lot of free space on the walls, even the students' own work should be put up with some thought. Often, there are better gallery spaces at school than simply on the wall of the classroom.

All visual material is not necessary to be kept out all the time. The periodic table of elements does not improve one's learning of languages, and the world map does not help students focus on mathematics. Visual aids can also be kept out based on individual needs, through differentiation. For example, all students may not need to see examples of how letters are drawn on the walls, if only one student needs that visual aid. A reference for drawing letters can be placed on the student's desk or attached to a partition next to them. For example, a plastic pocket attached to the desk can help with changing materials based on the lesson and learning objectives.

Differentiating the physical learning environment

- Make sure the basics, such as lighting and air conditioning, are sorted out.
- Actively verbalise the learning environment and its differentiated use.
- Choose the seats of the students based on individual needs: near the teacher, next to a talented student or away from distractions, such as the door or windows.
- Try different kinds of seating arrangements in class: in groups, pairs, or independently.
- Make sure that the classroom is clean and that the materials on the wall are straight and intact.
- Make sure that all things have a named place in the classroom.
- Eliminate unnecessary stimulating materials, such as posters and pictures on the walls.
- Think carefully about the use of visual aids.
- Arrange different kinds of learning stations or spaces for group work, quiet reading and independent working.
- Utilise the different spaces at school: one can equip different classrooms on the same grade level differently.

THE PSYCHO-SOCIAL LEARNING ENVIRONMENT

The atmosphere and relationships that relate to learning can be harder to see than the physical learning environment. However, they are likely to have a bigger effect on learning than the physical learning environment. Differentiating the psycho-social learning environment is also considerably harder than differentiating the physical learning environment, since sometimes they are outside the teacher's sphere of influence. For example, it is hard to affect the situation a student has at home. However, certain basic things in the classroom need to be considered, so that the environment supports learning psycho-socially. Next, we will explore the psycho-social learning environment from the perspective of differentiation.

By the psychological learning environment, we mean the feelings and emotions that are present in a learning situation and that can be positive or negative. A typical feeling that negatively affects the learning situation is being nervous, which can occur, for example, due to bullying in the class. A positive feeling can be the safe and relaxed atmosphere in the classroom, which creates peace and enthusiasm in the students, thus improving their capability to learn. Especially in lower grades, the teacher has a central role in creating and upholding a positive psychological learning environment in the classroom.

Learning does not happen in a vacuum, and the people with whom and through whom one learns are a big part of the learning situation. For example, if there is distrust between the teacher and the parents, this will affect learning negatively. On the other hand, a working educational cooperation between the home and the school aids learning, even when faced with challenges. With the social learning environment, we refer to relationships that affect learning, as well as the interaction between people who take part in learning. At school, the social learning environment includes teachers and students, but also the whole faculty of the school. In addition, the social learning environment is strongly affected by the parents and family of the student. Thinking about it in a wider perspective, the social learning environment includes all the cooperative bodies of the school that somehow affect the student's school life, such as youth workers and public librarians.

CREATE A GOOD ATMOSPHERE

In the classroom, it is important to safeguard the central psycho-social requirements for learning. These include, for example, a safe atmosphere in the classroom, and good, trusting interaction between students, the teacher, and parents. Keeping in contact with the home, immediate intervention in all bullying, and creating clear boundaries and rules in the classroom are central factors that make a safe and trusting atmosphere possible.

A good atmosphere does not appear or stay in the classroom by itself. It needs to be worked for. It is easy to imagine how learning in the classroom becomes difficult if a student has to be afraid of others laughing at them if they get a question wrong. Commenting on and laughing at other students' answers repeat themselves. If Rasmus' answers have been laughed at before, he is likely to act the same way towards others. A zero tolerance policy is the only right answer in regard to bullying and commenting on other students' answers. It is good to be systematic. It is important to intervene even in the smallest of situations, because it sends the students a message. Not intervening or not giving attention to situations like these are instances of silent acceptance of bullying. It would be important to spread the culture of intervention to all adults and the whole school. Thus, the common pedagogical philosophy of all staff is important. Common rules are meaningful only when everyone sticks to them.

IF NEEDED, DIFFERENTIATE BREAKS AND FREE MOMENTS

Breaks are meant to relax after learning. For students like Rasmus, who need support in social situation, breaks are the most difficult and taxing moment of the day. During breaks, the support of an adult can also be scarce. Breaks make up a considerable portion of the school day, and thus, they have a large effect on not only the psycho-social learning environment, but also directly on learning.

Sometimes at school, one hears teachers wanting to focus on their basic task, which is teaching. One can think of teaching occurring only during a lesson in the classroom, but in reality, the whole school day is vital in learning, especially when considering it from the perspective of the psycho-social learning environment. Sometimes at school, it is forgotten that some students need individual support and differentiation also during breaks, and that it should be primarily supplied by the teacher. This does not mean that the teacher should be outside with the children during each break, although sometimes this kind of support can be justified and yield considerable results. Nevertheless, differentiation should be kept in mind even during the free moments at school.

In many schools, breaks are differentiated without even noticing. In a school with both primary and secondary grades in the same building, younger and older students can have different break times. Also, some play equipment can be reserved for certain age groups. Similar differentiation can be extended to individual students. During breaks, social skills and abilities develop almost without noticing. Sometimes the student needs the physical presence of an adult during break. This time spent together will be fruitful in the classroom. It increases the teacher's knowledge of the student and strengthens the trust between the teacher and the student.

While differentiating breaks and free time, it is important to make sure that each student knows what kind of behaviour is expected of them during free situations. Verbalisation of things, situations, and actions can help with setting individual goals. For a student in need of support, it is good to offer readily available solutions for different problem situations. For example, the student can be advised to come indoors or to find a teacher on break duty every time they do not know what to do in a situation.

Sometimes, with a student like Rasmus, one can arrange an indoor break in order to avoid fights with others. The student can spend one break per day indoors to allow for appropriate time spent outdoors. With this arrangement, the goal is to guarantee the student a successful day without fights or failures. One does not have to spend an indoor break only sitting in the classroom. Instead, one can go to the gym with the student to score some goals, for example, if the space is available. The teacher can drink their coffee or grade papers there, while keeping an eye on the student. In this situation, the bond between the teacher and the student is strengthened, when the teacher has time to pay attention to the individual student. Often, it is the student behaving the most challengingly who needs the moral support of an adult. In addition, one can ask some classmates to play with Rasmus during the indoor break. In a small group, Rasmus can practice his social skills, and the teacher can support the situation. This kind of arrangement improves the interactions between students like Rasmus and other children, thus affecting the social environment of the classroom positively.

The teacher should remember that they are not alone at school, even during breaks. If an aggressive student like Rasmus needs individual support from an adult during break, individual break monitoring can be arranged between familiar adults at school. During one break, the students can spend time outside with the teacher, while another break can be spent indoors with a learning assistant. A student can also help the caretaker with their chores around the school. As the student's social skills get better, they can simply be asked to report to the teacher.

The break area can first be reduced strongly, and this can be later widened as the student progresses in their social skills. In autumn, breaks can be spent at arm's length from the teacher, but as skills develop, play can move as far as the teacher can see. As the student gains age and skills, other students can be used in differentiation. Students in the class can have break partners or breaks can be spent with a peer mentor. One should immediately reward the student's success in behaving well by giving positive feedback. Short-term goals can be monitored by accumulating stickers or stamps on a card after a successful break. When students have collected a prescribed number of stickers, this can lead to a fun activity chosen by the students. Positive feedback is essential. However, it is good to remind the students that they could also lose a gained bonus. Using different incentives is shown more in Chapter 5.

In the beginning of the school year, students should be played with and taught how to play in a group. Some students need more support in this than others. Old school yard games, like duck-duck-goose, are popular among primary schoolers almost without exceptions. However, not all students know how to play them. In games and guided activities, students like Catherine, who are older and socially talented, can be utilised. The whole school taking part in collective break time activities creates the community spirit, strengthens the feeling of belonging, and improves the atmosphere of the whole school.

PREPARE FOR, ENSURE AND DIFFERENTIATE IN TRANSITIONS AND FREE MOMENTS

Most often, arguments and fights at school occur during breaks and the so-called free moments, in which the student is expected to act in a certain way independently. Transitions from one place to another are especially volatile. However, these situations are the easiest to prepare for. Considering and differentiating free moments creates a safe atmosphere at school, which benefits learning.

Free transitions and moments are created naturally within the school day. Sometimes, as teachers, we can create them with our own actions. Students come in after a break right after the break ends. However, the teacher sometimes is not in the classroom when the bell rings. Unnecessary tardiness creates unnecessary moments in which fights and difficulties ensue.

The easiest way to differentiate transitions is preparation. For many students who need special support, routines create safety and breaking them can feel scary or threatening. All transitions or exceptions can be prepared for by differentiation. The student can be individually prepared for a change of schedule or programme prior to the moment it happens. The schedule can also be written down for the student. In some cases, a visual aid, for example a picture, can be necessary.

Sometimes a student may need individual direction in an exceptional situation. This extra support can be provided by the teacher or learning assistant, or even a classmate or a student from a higher grade. All arrangements strive to make everyone feel safe in the classroom.

Routine transitions do not require similar preparation as single exceptions in teaching. These routine transitions are lunch time, breaks or a change of classrooms during the school day. A student's coat can be hanging in the classroom so that putting it on can happen under the teacher's watchful eye to avoid bickering in the corridor. Sometimes the student in need of differentiation can leave for their break a few minutes before or after others. Older students often know how to take care of their schedule individually. However, with small students or in situations where the teacher cannot be there to support, the transition can be scheduled by using a mobile phone or even an egg timer. Out of our example students, Rasmus should be let out a few minutes before others so he can put his coat on in peace. When the phone alarm goes off, Rasmus will know to come in, even if the bell has not rung for the other students.

Differentiating breaks and free moments

- Make sure that the student knows what is expected of them.
- Prepare for changes and go through them with the student in preparation.
- Let the students know about transitions or changes: 'In five minutes, we will go to the cafeteria.'

... continued

... continued

- Make sure that the student gets support during transitions, either from the teacher, learning assistant, classmate or a peer mentor.
- Offer prescribed solutions to difficult situations: What will you do if there is a fight? Who can you go to for advice?
- Start and end the lesson on time.
- Individually put boundaries on the student's break time, area and activities.
- Remember clear consequences if unwanted behaviour occurs, which are known to the students as well.
- Make sure the students spend their breaks with the teacher, learning assistant, a classmate or a peer mentor.
- Name permanent break partners.
- Make sure that there are enough activities during break. Teach students how to play. Have older students take part in playing with the younger ones.
- Let the student spend some of their breaks indoors, but make sure they get enough exercise during the day.

GROUP STUDENTS TOGETHER SYSTEMATICALLY THROUGHOUT THE SCHOOL YEAR

Different social exercises that let the students and the teacher get to know one another are often used when teachers start with a new group. However, social relationships are not created or kept alive by themselves, and not all students are as talented at creating them. Knowing your students is central to all differentiation, including the differentiation of the psycho-social learning environment. It is vital when creating a safe learning environment that the class has been grouped together well and that the students know one another.

This could be the content of one lesson per week. Grouping exercises do not only improve the social atmosphere of the classroom, but also increase the teacher's knowledge of the students, which helps with differentiating the learning environment.

FORM PAIRS AND GROUPS UNDER THE DIRECTION OF THE TEACHER

Many of us probably remember that PE lesson in which two students picked the most popular students in their teams, one by one. This certainly did not help those students' learning who were the last to be picked. Furthermore, the best end product does not always get made by a group of friends. When the teacher picks the pairs and groups, they can purposefully differentiate not only the content, but also the psycho-social learning environment. The most quiet and timid student should not necessarily be put to work together with the loudest, most socially domineering student. However, in the optimal situation, a socially talented, outgoing student can certainly help a more reserved student to learn social interaction skills.

Pairing up or forming groups under the teacher's instruction does not mean that the student can never choose with whom to work. However, forming pairs and groups should be a conscious and well thought-out process, which supports learning objectives. By consciously selecting working partners, one can differentiate the learning situation based on the students' needs. It is good to remember that the formation of working groups and pairs takes time. It may be justified to change groups and partners each lesson, but this serves a different purpose than long-lived pair or group work. Starting work in a new group develops social skills if the students already grasp the basic principles of pair and group work. With the correct grouping and long-term work, these skills can also be developed together with other, content-based learning objectives.

VARY YOUR TEACHING GROUPS

Learning difficulties and strengths are unique. They are not always concentrated on one thing, or even on one subject. A linguistically talented student might need more support in mathematics, while a student who struggles with basic calculations in mathematics may be very good at geometry. Students also learn, grow, and develop constantly, and the social structure of the classroom changes. Permanent skill sets or a permanent divide into weak and talented students do not belong in differentiation.

The psycho-social learning environment

– Ensure the safety and positive atmosphere of the learning environment. This is a prerequisite for differentiation.
– Always intervene in all kinds of bullying.
– Remember to consider free moments and transitions.
– Form pairs and groups with the leadership of the teacher.
– Vary learning groups based on learning objectives.

Students can be grouped together during lessons based on skills, personality, work style, or an area of interest. This variety in learning groups helps students both keep up and create new relationships. This helps the psychological and social learning environments in the classroom. Pairs and groups should naturally be varied purposefully, as the teacher sees fit, based on the students' needs and the learning objectives. Different groupings is further explored in Chapter 3. The learning environment of the classroom, not to mention the whole school, cannot be changed at once. The most important thing is to differentiate the learning environment one step at a time.

Tips to remedy the starting point

GRADE 1: SAM

- Ensure a workstation in a place from which Sam can see the classroom quickly, for example, in the back of the classroom.
- Direct attention during quiet working, using a partition, or perhaps headphones or earmuffs.
- Attach individual working instructions onto the workstation.
- Remember visual aids in the instructions.
- Give up the teacher's desk in the classroom.
- Remove named desks when they are not necessary.

GRADE 3: RASMUS

- Ensure clearly named places for all things.
- Utilise indoor breaks.
- Prepare for free moments.
- Reserve time for team spirit and activities, first one lesson per week (see Chapter 8).
- With the students, agree on a reward for the wanted behaviours and good work.
- Set goals so that they are achievable and not too big.

GRADE 5: AMY

- Seat near the teacher or a responsible student.
- Only keep things that are used daily in the classroom.
- Remove all excess visual aids from the walls.
- Give individual written instructions for working.

GRADE 9: CATHERINE

- Systematically group the class during different lessons.
- Use Catherine on lower grades, for example as a peer mentor.
- Vary teaching groups based on objectives.
- Make different working methods and individual progress possible in the classroom.

5. TEACHING METHODS

The starting point

GRADE 1: SAM

During lessons, Sam does not focus on instructions and does the wrong things because of this. A whole lesson is too hard for Sam to concentrate, and he reacts to this by disturbing teaching and the other students' work. Sam especially dislikes handwritten activities, and even the smallest noise or movement makes him lose focus. Sam cannot sit still for long, and leaves his seat often, disturbing other students.

GRADE 3: RASMUS

Rasmus likes working in pairs or groups during lessons. However, he wants that things always go his way, and when there is a conflict, he gets angry easily. Other students in the class are afraid of Rasmus and would not want to work with him. Rasmus does not have challenges in learning, but there is a lot to improve in his working methods and social skills. Handwritten work is abhorrent and the defiance and aggression manifest as improper behaviour towards both the teacher and the classmates.

GRADE 5: AMY

Amy feels that it is hard to understand and remember the teacher's verbal instructions. Because of this, she often takes a lot of time getting started in her work. In class, the students often work on the same thing at the same time. It is hard for Amy to finish the given tasks during the lesson, so she has to complete them at home. She often gets a lot of homework because of this, and she spends a great amount of time doing them at home.

GRADE 9: CATHERINE

Catherine manages to finish all work way before the others. The teacher usually does not have any more challenging activities for her. The rest of the class, Catherine doodles in her notebooks or reads a book she brought from home. She feels like things go too slowly at school. The homework is the same as other students', and she gets through them easily.

In this chapter, we consider differentiation in teaching methods, which mean different practices that support the students' learning. Each of us certainly have some methods we have found beneficial in our tool box, which we have used more than others. However, we do often stay too far within our comfort zone when it comes to teaching methods, and we do not even come to think about something new. The method that fits the teacher does not necessarily support the student's learning. The functional and active teaching style Sam loves might be terrible for Amy. In differentiated instruction, one should specifically vary different teaching methods, so that all kinds of students are considered better. In the beginning of the chapter, we take a look at general things regarding differentiated instruction. After this, we present a list of differentiation practices that we have personally used in our own teaching.

THE PRINCIPLES OF DIFFERENTIATED INSTRUCTION

In a differentiated classroom, teaching should be approached by considering the individuality of the students. Thus, differentiation is included also in the basic, general things in teaching. All students benefit from certain teaching practices, but for many struggling students they are a prerequisite for successful education. Next, we will take a look at what we consider to be the most central elements of a differentiated classroom, which are *study skills, instruction-giving, individual progress, homework, structure, incentives* and *learning materials.*

TEACH STUDY SKILLS AND INDEPENDENT DIRECTION

In differentiated instruction, the student's study skills, or the strategies and techniques the student uses to learn, are highlighted. Different study techniques are emphasised in different subjects. For example, in subjects like history, one uses strategies based on reading, whereas foreign languages can be learned more through hearing comprehension strategies. In addition to subject-specific techniques and strategies, students should also practice general study skills. We will talk about reading-specific study skills more in Chapter 8.

We all have individual habits and preferences when it comes to learning. However, students are not always conscious of their own habits, and they can be stuck in certain ways of doing things that are not very effective. Students can, for example, start to read chapters in a book straight from the start without taking a look at the pictures or subtitles first, or start to translate a text in a foreign language word-by-word. In class, one should practice and periodically review different study techniques and think with the students how they feel and how they improve learning. It is important to find the study methods that each student finds natural. The teacher should actively consider these in their teaching, and offer opportunities to practice those methods. For example, a student like Amy might benefit from taking notes by taking pictures or recordings, instead of writing them down on a page (see Chapter 6).

With study skills, the students' self-direction is emphasised, especially with those students in higher grades. In a differentiated classroom, it is good to teach students initiative and certain practices that benefit studying and make classroom work smoother. These practices include reading instructions well, paying attention to the work, checking the work carefully and moving onto the next task independently. For example, in the classroom, one can agree on a practice where students can start reading a book or do extra activities from the back of the workbook after they have finished the necessary tasks. Self-direction can be practiced, for example, by contractual project work, which we will touch upon later in this chapter.

One should spend a lot of time practising self-direction and study skills before they become automatic and natural. The smaller the students are, the weaker their readiness is for self-direction. With determined practice, even the youngest of students can become very self-directive. For example, even first-graders can learn certain steps for working, such as reading a chapter independently and following up with completing the activities. One should note that self-direction can also be difficult, even for older students. With them, it is good to practice it, starting small, for example by taking out the correct books at first. With low-achieving students, one can use action cards to practice self-direction. These action cards can be found in Appendix 5. The appendix also includes empty cards, which the teacher can fill in based on the situations they face in their teaching, with their specific students. Activity cards can be made with the student, for example by acting out the actions and taking pictures of them. Then, for example, the teacher and student can think about what is included in silent working, and what a student looks like while working silently in their seat.

When practising study skills and self-direction, all students' learning is supported. In addition, this serves differentiation by freeing the teacher's resources to direct students individually, if needed. It is important that the students learn how to use the study methods best suited for them even at home. Once again, it is good to involve parents in this. For example, a parents' evening could be themed to be all about study skills and considering them at home. That way, for example, studying for tests becomes more efficient.

Tips for supporting active learning

- Be determined to go over study skills and their importance in learning.
- Practice different methods and direct your students to reflect on how they work for them.
- Teach students different study techniques individually, based on their needs. For example, one can take notes by taking pictures or recordings.
- Teach students self-direction. Utilise the action cards in Appendix 5.
- Teach parents about study skills and how to support their children with them.

GIVE CLEAR AND SUPPORTED INSTRUCTIONS

Teachers instruct students multiple times per school day in different situations. The most common way is to give spoken instructions to the whole class, for example when letting students know what they should do next. Many students can pick out the most important information in the instructions, but there are students like Sam or Amy in the class who have a hard time understanding verbal instructions. Some students cannot keep up with long-winded instructions with multiple parts because of bad concentration, for some, it is a matter of remembering them, and some students simply do not understand even when paying attention. Clear and supported instructions also benefit high-achieving students, since they free up resources for other work.

IMAGE 3. One should pay attention to the way one instructs and the clarity of communication

When giving instructions, it is important to make sure that every student is concentrating and paying attention to listening to instructions. Students should be taught to have eye contact to the teacher while instructions are given. Sitting in the front can help with getting and keeping eye contact. One can get the attention of students who have trouble concentrating by naming them before giving instructions. Students can also be taught a signal that marks a time when instructions are given. For example, one can ring a bell or lift up a flag as a signal for the need to listen very carefully. For some students, such as those with autism spectrum disorder, eye contact can be difficult. Knowing one's students helps to identify a student for whom eye contact is not a prerequisite for concentration.

One should also think about one's stance and place in the class, so that one does not give instructions while in motion or sitting behind the teacher's desk. The best way to instruct is standing up, clearly in view, from the front of the room. One should also concentrate on one's speech. One can keep up the students' attention better by varying one's tone, pitch, intonation, and register of voice. Monotonous or boring speech can make students lose focus. Instead of trying to talk loudly over everyone, one can try speaking a little more quietly. A sudden change can make students focus better. It is always important to make sure the instructions have been received. It is good to support the verbal instructions by body language, including gestures and facial expressions. This helps students understand and remember the instructions better.

In general, it is necessary to pay attention to clarity when giving instructions. Many students in need of differentiation have a poor working memory, so keeping many things in mind at once is hard. Instructions should be made as simple as possible, and to comprise only a few actions. The student often only remembers the beginning and the end of long instructions, so the big picture remains unseen. Clear instructions benefit the whole class, but for low-achievers, they are a prerequisite for smooth education.

It is good to teach students strategies to support their memory. They should be actively practiced in class, so that they will work in practice. For example, multi-step instructions are easier to remember when the student can see the number of steps the instructions contain. The student can be asked to put up the correct number of fingers to support their memory. This way, they can follow whether they have completed all instructions more easily. Some students need individual instructions, which can be given either before or after commonly announced instructions. Sometimes it is useful to instruct pre-emptively. For example, before break, students can be briefly told about the topic and work methods used in next class, so they have an easier time following instructions in the beginning of next class.

Instructions should be supported by text or pictures. Each instruction during a lesson is unnecessary to depict, but, for example, one should use pictures when introducing a new type of work. If making pictures seems like too much work, one can draw a simple series of drawings on the board to support the instructions. One can also use ready-made software and action cards (see Appendix 5). Especially for immigrant students and small children, visual support is often necessary. It is safe for the student to check the pictures what they need to do next. The clear illustration of different steps helps students to understand their work better, which improves their self-knowledge and self-direction. Using pictures or written support helps the whole class, so for some instructions, the teacher can put the pictures on the board for everyone to see. Alternatively, illustrated instructions can be only given to individual students. The illustrated instructions can also be put in writing in a foreign language, so it can work as a tool for language acquisition for students who would otherwise not need illustrated instructions.

It is important to make sure that everyone has understood the instructions and know what is meant to happen. A good way to do this is to ask one of the students to repeat the instructions in their own words. This way, the whole class gets to hear them again. To best way to find out the most effective method to give instructions to your students is through trial and error, as well as your knowledge of them. However, it is important that the instructions are always given in the same way, so that the way instructions are given will become familiar. Then, each student can learn to focus on the important things.

Tips for giving instructions
- Make sure that the students focus on listening to instructions.
- Focus on your own stance and use of voice.
- Give concise and clear instructions.
- If necessary, support instructions with writing or pictures.
- Make sure that everyone has understood the instructions.
- If needed, give individual instructions.

MAKE INDIVIDUAL PROGRESS POSSIBLE

Usually at school, everyone studies the same things in the same way. Some feel like considerably different work on different topics can contribute to feeling different, making differentiation too obvious. The teacher can also feel like the communal and social sides of learning are forgotten if all students are offered individualised work. However, in this line of thought, one can see a certain stiffness in school culture. We are used to everyone doing the same thing at the same time at school. In differentiation, one specifically creates a culture that allows for and normalises different students doing different things at different times. In one's own classroom, one can start to build a working culture in which work can be more flexible. Students do not have to do the same things all the time, and the boundaries of the lesson should not be as strict. We wrote about the importance of individual challenges and verbalising learning objectives in Chapter 4.

Differentiation does not mean that students work alone all the time. For example, when one teaches new content, this should be done together as a class. However, there are many moments at school when work could be more individual and flexible than it is now. It is not wise to stick to a certain length of the lesson with students like Sam, for whom a whole lesson is too long to work on one thing. With a student like Sam, one should start with small steps and keep work time short at first. It is important to offer experiences of success for students, and to avoid the student having to constantly struggle to reach their limits. Of course, the goal of the whole class is to work for a certain time, but sometimes a student cannot do this. Then, it is good to differentiate the amount of time spent on working, based on individual goals.

In practice, we have noticed that, for example, while teaching mathematics, one completes one chapter of the workbook per lesson. The teacher carries on, even though all students have not understood the topic of last class. One should progress more individualistically in teaching mathematics, so that a student could do problems they need to practice most at that time. In special needs and multi-grade classrooms, this is commonplace, and students can be studying even five different topics at once. We do not mean that students should always be working on their individual activities in class, but one can try to add even a little consideration of the individual needs of the class. In mathematics, one can progress with teaching with the whole class during most lessons, but in one lesson, let students work on topics in which they need the most practice. It is good to stop and consider whether the obstacle for individual progress is time, resources or even the whole school's working culture. Are we simply used to doing things a certain way without considering or testing different practices?

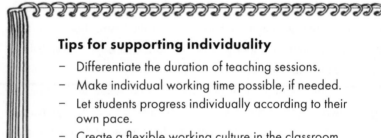

Tips for supporting individuality
- Differentiate the duration of teaching sessions.
- Make individual working time possible, if needed.
- Let students progress individually according to their own pace.
- Create a flexible working culture in the classroom.

CONSIDER INDIVIDUALITY IN HOMEWORK

Homework is an essential part of a student's life. Unfortunately, many students have a hard time getting through them. For some reason, they have not marked their homework properly, the books are left at school or they cannot complete them because they do not know how, have the energy or remember to do them at home.

Even when assigning homework, one needs to differentiate. Teachers have a habit of assigning homework in the end of the lesson, when the students' minds are already on break mode. One could try to assign homework in the beginning of the lesson, when the students have an easier time focusing. Simply telling the students verbally is not enough, and homework should be visually present. For example, writing homework down on the board benefits everyone, and is a good support for those who need it.

For some students, reading the homework instructions off the board is not enough support, and they still need more help marking their homework. Sometimes, one can use peer support in this, so that the person sitting next to the student can help them mark their homework. One can use a homework notebook, in which the student or teacher marks down the homework for the day. The notebook can help monitor the progress of the student, both at home and at school. It also makes the student's progress known to the student themselves. It is also good to check that a student who tends to forget their homework only has those books in their bag that they will need for homework. Sometimes students carry all of their books in their bag, which makes it harder to remember which homework the students have. One can ask the parent to put a check mark in the notebook when the homework is done. In collaboration with the home, one can focus the homework of a low-achieving student on a certain subject, so that it is easier to monitor. Then, the child can have a little daily piece of homework in mathematics or language and literature. It makes it easier to remember if the homework is spread out over the whole week, even if the subject is only taught on one day of the week. The student can be asked to read out loud for 15 minutes per day, to learn three new words in a foreign language or to complete a times table work sheet.

For some students, common homework can be too difficult, and they can even take hours completing it. This does not serve differentiation, and one should consider the student's goals when assigning homework. What homework could help the student progress according to their individual objectives? With some students, it is good to differentiate both the level and the amount of homework. For example, in mathematics, a low-achiever can be assigned only a few written problems, and in foreign languages ask to write five words in the notebook, instead of all the words in the chapter's vocabulary. If Amy's goal in English is to learn certain words and sentences, mainly orally, one should not make her complete a lot of written work as homework.

Individualised homework can be assigned in the beginning or middle of the lesson, if the end of the lesson seems too hectic for differentiation. The student can also be asked to choose their own homework, since it gives the student more agency and responsibility for completing it.

For some students, it is good to reconsider homework altogether. If going to school and completing work there are difficult and burdening, one should not give more work to be completed at home. Instead, one can agree on certain tasks that have to be completed during class, and this can be the student's objective. After completing them, they can stay homework-less for the day. This motivates the student to work harder during class. The objective of the lesson is good to be made clear to the students even in the beginning of the lesson.

Sometimes, parents need differentiated instruction to help their child with homework. In some homes, all energy is put into completing the last bits of homework. Parents can be instructed to help the child, but it is good to remember that it is the child's work to complete. If the student cannot complete the homework independently, or it takes too long, it is a message to the teacher that the homework is too challenging and that they need to differentiate the homework accordingly. A good rule of thumb is that homework should only take an hour of the day. In the beginning of school, 20-30 minutes is enough. It is hard to give a general time limit, because students and their working style and rhythm are unique. However, one should compare the time spent on homework with the time they spend in class. Can we expect a child to work as hard at home without the teacher's support as they do in a lesson?

Consistency in homework is more important than time at primary level. Of course, one spends more time on homework as one grows older, but this should be in relation to the weekly work time. If a student studies 30 hours per week at school, it is almost as much as the weekly hours an adult works in their job. Homes can be instructed to make sure the student takes a break in between doing their homework, perhaps by using an egg timer. One should also inform the parents about the teacher's homework assigning practices, since parents can sometimes be timid about asking for help with challenges.

Many teachers are unnecessarily afraid about the other students' attitudes towards someone getting assigned different homework. As we wrote in the previous chapter, students acknowledge and identify differences in class. Differentiation by itself creates a school culture that cherishes and respects difference. Individual homework can become a norm that does not cause negative experiences of being different, even for the low-achieving students.

Tips for differentiating homework

- Assign homework at an appropriate time during the lesson, either in the beginning, middle or the end.
- Mark homework somewhere everyone can see it, for example on the edge of the board.
- Assign homework based on individual objectives. Think about whether all students should even get homework. Agree on the amount of work a student should have between all subject teachers at secondary school level.
- Assign the same or similar homework for a long period of time.
- Use individual support methods, such as peer support or a homework notebook.
- Offer parents tips in supporting homework.

REMEMBER CLARITY, ORGANISATION, AND PERMANENCE

In addition to differentiation, structure is a word that is often used while talking about good teaching. Often, it is only spoken about, and not practiced enough in teaching. However, structure is an integral part of differentiation, since it helps students section their work and discern the important things from all information. Characteristics of structured teaching are clarity, organisation and permanence.

Structure can be practiced in the classroom in many ways. For many students, it is hard to understand the structure of the day, and they need the adult's support and direction. Low-achieving students in particular benefit from clear routines that structure and direct the procession of the day. For example, checking one's homework or leaving for lunch should always happen in the same, familiar way.

In teaching, one should pay attention especially to the beginnings and ends of lessons. Lessons should always be started clearly, in the same way, so that students learn to prepare for situations and regulate their behaviour during them. The objective of the lesson should be clarified in the beginning of the lesson. Similarly, the endings of the lesson are also important in terms of structure. Sometimes, the lesson almost dies down by itself and students start to pack their things and prepare for break, which can seem unorganised for certain students. Lessons should be ended with specific routines. It is good to go over the content that was learned during the lesson.

In order to structure the school day, it is good to have a daily schedule always visible in class. The schedule can be as detailed as necessary. Sometimes it is enough that the lessons of the day can be seen. Some students benefit from also seeing breaks, transitions or more specific steps of the lessons. Especially with little students, an illustrated schedule will benefit the whole class and should be visible to all. With older students, a written or illustrated schedule can sometimes be placed on individual students' desks.

Many students have a hard time understanding the passing of time during a single lesson. Especially in lower grade levels, one hears questions like 'How long until the lesson ends?' or 'When's break time?' The student cannot concentrate on work, if it feels endless. Even as adults, we can focus on something better if we know how much time we have to spend on the task. If students can see the time left, they can focus better until the end. For example, using a 'time timer' is a good way to depict the procession of the lesson to a student who cannot tell time. The time that should be spent working should be marked in red, and the students can clearly see the red getting smaller and smaller as time passes by. If you do not have access to one, you can mark a place on a normal clock with tape, to which the long hand of the clock needs to get to, depicting when the students can stop working.

Tips for creating structure

- Hold onto certain basic routines.
- Focus on the beginnings and ends of the lesson.
- Verbalise what happens during the lesson. Let the students know the goal of the lesson in the beginning and debrief what happened during the class at the end.
- Keep an illustrated daily schedule visible.
- Demonstrate the passing of time during lessons and the school day.
- Structure the students' school day individually, if necessary.

REWARD SUCCESS

Every one of us wants to get thanked and recognised for good performance. Especially for a low-achieving student, it is important to remember to give positive feedback every time it is applicable, since challenges at school often affect the student's confidence negatively. Praise is not the purpose, since positive feedback under false pretences completely undoes the thanks from the teacher. However, it is important to differentiate the requirements for praise. For example, a student like Rasmus who has behavioural issues deserves praise for a day without violence, whereas for others this is a given.

It is important to remember small steps in positive feedback. The student's individual goals need to be set so that they are able to be reached, and one can give deserved positive feedback for this. Individual goals should be verbalised to the whole class. In this case, the reward or praise does not seem arbitrary or unequal. If the goal of an aggressive student has been not hitting anyone, the positive feedback should be given specifically for that, even though he or she has been in a verbal argument. This does not mean that calling each other names is acceptable or that one should not intervene. However, individual goals should be remembered even in a conflict.

Verbal praise is not always enough to reward or motivate the student at school. Concrete reward systems can be used in these cases. They especially motivate younger students, but, if the right reward is found, this can also work for older students. This reward system could be tested with Sam or Rasmus, who have trouble working and behaving well. The reward should be something the student really likes, and the student should have a say in the matter. As a reward, the student can, for example, pick some motivating activity that does not bother the other students, which they can do in the end of the lesson. Individual rewards can be very different, as long as they are easily arrangeable, such as time to play on the computer or reading a comic book.

Different sticker and stamp arrangements work well with young students. The student can get a sticker for every successful lesson, and after collecting enough stickers, a reward will be given. This reward system, like all other support arrangements, should be agreed on with the home. For example, stickers collected at school can lead to something fun at home. The most effective method is to expect similar behaviour both at school and at home. If collaboration with the home is difficult, the importance of the school and the teacher is highlighted.

When using rewards, it is important to consider the unique needs and situation of the student. With some, it is important to focus on the goals of a single lesson, or even a shorter teaching session. For others, the goals can spread over a whole day or even a week. Goals should also be changed as skills grow. However, at first, one should start small, with short-term goals. The important thing is to make the goals reachable, in order to set the student up for success. For example, for a student like Sam, who has trouble focusing, the first goal could be working quietly for ten minutes. Once again, we come back to the culture of the classroom. If students are used to acknowledging individual arrangements in class, they will also accept that some of them are allowed to work for a shorter period of time.

Tips for rewarding students' progress
- Differentiate giving feedback.
- Set goals so that it is possible to give positive feedback.
- Try a reward system.
- Let the student have a say in the reward.
- Collaborate with the home.
- Start with goals that are easily reachable.

CONSIDER INDIVIDUALITY WHEN PICKING AND USING LEARNING MATERIALS

Differentiation can be approached both from the perspective of individual and common learning material. Often, if feels like there are not enough time and resources to prepare or acquire individual material. However, one does not have to give up, since differentiation can be done at a group level, using the same materials. Then, students are given different goals for their individual work, and the work they produce can be on a different level than the others. Open assignments, such as projects and presentations, work best in individually completing a communal piece of work. However, even written work sheets and problems from the workbook can also be differentiated based on the needs of the student.

Students' uniqueness has been considered lately when making learning materials. Problems and questions in new school books have sometimes been marked with different difficulty levels, which helps to direct differentiation.

However, teacher still feel like textbooks are too uniform and do not serve purposeful differentiation. Pre-differentiated learning materials give tips for differentiation, but are still uniform at their own level, so they do not always work for the lowest achieving students. Although learning materials are often uniform, they can be used differently with different students. Students can be asked to only complete some of the questions or allow them to answer with single words, instead of full sentences. It can be justified for students like Amy to only read the summaries from science and history textbooks.

In our work, we have run into situations in which teachers require all students to complete the two-page chapter in the mathematics workbook during one lesson. If they cannot manage this, the rest will be left for homework, including any other homework assigned for that lesson. For some, this may seem as equal treatment, but this does not take the students' individual skill levels into account at all. If one compares completing the pages in the mathematics workbook with running around a track, it is easy to see that Usain Bolt can complete his round much faster than us. If differentiation was to occur, everyone would run as far as they can for 15 minutes, and it would not matter how far the others run. By doing this, everyone's fitness can improve at their own pace.

The same principle should be practiced in class. It is important to remember that for some students it is as hard to complete one problem as it is for other students to complete the whole two pages. Many teachers think that a low-achieving student like Amy needs a lot of practice and revision, and thus benefits from completing the whole two-page chapter. However, one can approach the situation from the perspective of the student's motivation and wellbeing. It is certainly more supportive for the student if they feel like they can complete the given tasks and that they are not always behind or work too slowly.

At its foundation, offering individual assignments for students better serves efficient learning. However, it is challenging if there are many students in need of individual material and very little pre-made material available. One should use all channels available to fix this problem. One can use workbooks from different grade levels. For example, in Finland, language and literature and mathematics follow a spiral structure in which content and themes are repeated at different breadth and depth on different grade levels. For example, it might be useful for a student like Amy to go through lower grade level books when learning fractions or grammar. Furthermore, a high-achieving student like Catherine could benefit from getting work from higher grade levels.

In everyday life, there does not seem to be enough time for making and finding personalised material. As a solution, students can be grouped in three or two groups, and use materials for two levels. This is not overwhelmingly burdening, but takes the students' needs better into account than only using one book. One can also ask for help from other teachers with making and finding differentiated materials. This way, by sharing materials, a single teacher's workload is not increased. We will explore different differentiated supportive material and its flexible use in Chapter 6.

Differentiation with common material
- Set individual goals.
- Ask for work to a different standard.
- Do not demand the student to complete all problems, for example in mathematics.

Differentiation with individualised material
- Utilise materials from different grade levels.
- Group students together in two groups and use two levels of materials.

DIFFERENTIATING WORK METHODS IN PRACTICE

At its core, differentiation is personalised, and thus, practices that apply to it can change student-to-student. However, we have noticed that starting differentiation with certain practices makes it easier. Next, we will show a few central teaching practices that are apt for differentiated instruction. We will also give examples for how to consider the individuality of each student while using those practices. The practices we have chosen are *independent work, contractual project work, station work* and *projects*.

INDEPENDENT WORK

One of the most typical modes of working at school is independent work, where students sit on their seats and work independently. While differentiating independent work, factors related to individual progress and learning materials are highlighted. However, work can also be differentiated in other areas. For example, for students like Sam, it is hard to concentrate on independent work, even though the classroom would be quiet and with little stimulation. Even the smallest sound or movement can distract some students. These students can be supported by the use of earmuffs, listening to music with headphones or allowing them to wear their hood up during work. We have found these to be good practices even for secondary school. In addition, one can reduce the number of visual stimuli by turning the desk towards the back wall for the duration of work, or by cornering the student's desk off by partitions. Often, students themselves notice how some practices benefit them and will start to ask for them independently. We will go over some practical tools in Chapter 6.

Especially for small students, sitting still can be very challenging, which makes independent work harder. With them, one can agree on a practice in which one is allowed to move around in class. Then, it is good to consider where the student sits in class. It is practical to place a student like Sam in the back of the classroom and agree with him that he can walk during the lesson, as long as he stays in the back of the room and does not bother anyone. For example, one can place the pencil-sharpening station in the back of the classroom to create natural movement. Furthermore, sometimes one can agree with a student that they can go walk around in the hallway, for example once during the lesson. Differentiating seating has been discussed in more detail in Chapter 4.

Nowadays, many students struggle with their executive functions. In other words, they have trouble with planning, starting, completing, and assessing their actions. This shows in the student's performance in class. The illustrated or written daily schedule mentioned while discussing the structure in teaching can help with the student's executive functions. However, many students benefit from even more detailed support. Small pictures on the student's desk can help get deeper into instructions. The steps to independent work, such as taking out the equipment, reading the assignment prompt, completing and checking the work, and moving onto the next task, can be illustrated on the desk. Similar things can be written down on the desk of an older student. It is good to practice setting and assessing the objectives of the lesson with all students. Setting goals for oneself and self-evaluation can also work well with secondary school students. One can direct a student like Catherine to set her goals higher than other students.

Often, one hears teachers refuse individualised practices, because they are afraid of how other students respond to them. Again, we return to the school's and classroom's working culture; if you create a culture that accepts and respects differences, students will understand the individual practices of others.

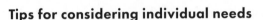

Tips for considering individual needs

- Try individualised solutions to support individual work, such as noise-cancelling headphones, listening to music or wearing a hood.
- Support the steps of independent work by pictures.
- Consider the seating arrangement.
- Allow the student to move during the lesson.
- Practice setting goals and assessing them with the students.

CONTRACTUAL PROJECT WORK

A good way to differentiate instruction is using the so-called contractual project work method. In this teaching method, the students are given a list of things to complete in a set time. Contractual projects can be done during one lesson, a day, a week or even a longer period. At first, it is good to start slowly, until this work method becomes familiar for the students. When trying contractual project work for the first times, work requires strong direction and monitoring. It is also good to remember that some students need strong adult support, even in the later stages. Adults should support especially the younger students to assess their own challenges. The contractual project work skills of the students will develop over time. One can reduce the level of the teacher's direction and monitoring as the student's skills increase. Too little support, or support that is ended too quickly, places the student in a situation in which the mountain of work seems overwhelming and the student cannot get started. In this case, support and direction needs to be increased in order to help the student structure their work and organise their workload.

The benefit of contractual project work is that time spent on a certain thing has not been limited according to the usual lesson durations. In contractual project work, the students can focus specifically on the things they need to practice most. Another benefit of contractual project work is that it enables the student to study the topic more in-depth. For example, students like Catherine can delve very deeply into a single topic, whereas lower achieving students can only look at the topic on surface level.

In contractual project work, the teacher can focus on supporting the low-achievers, whereas the higher achieving students can often work quite independently. Students can also be divided into pairs or groups, and they can decide on the order in which they complete the work within those groups. This arrangement makes peer support possible within differentiation. In optimally differentiated contractual project work, it would be good if the contracted work could be chosen based on the skill levels and areas of interest of the students.

The contractual project work can be started by allowing each student to make their own work plans. This includes the work that needs to be completed, in what time, along with the objectives of the work. For low-achieving students, contracts should be made under the leadership of the teacher so that the tasks and objectives remain realistic. It is likely that even the higher achieving students need a lot of direction and support in this. It is good to spend time on starting and reflecting on contractual project work with students. What went well? Where did I succeed? What should I do differently next time? Contractual project work develops executive functions, which was written about earlier in this chapter.

Tips for contractual project work

- Help students plan realistic work plans for contractual project work. Start with small workloads.
- Differentiate the amount of work and content of the contracts.
- Focus on directing the lowest achieving students.
- Utilise peer support in contractual project work.

STATION WORK

When differentiating with the whole group, station work works brilliantly. In this teaching method, students go around in pairs or groups and complete a different task or activity at each station. The benefit of station work is that the teacher can focus on directing the more challenging stations and support the lowest achieving students with them. Stations should be planned so that in some of them, the work is mechanical and not too challenging for the students. At independent stations, students must be able to work without the teacher's help. Different levels of work can also be available at those stations.

Station work can be done over one lesson, a day or even the whole week, based on how wide-ranging the stations are and what their contents are. One can vary the number of the stations according to the number of students. In the beginning or end, one can have a debriefing with the students, so that the time spent on the stations will be shorter. The activities at each station, and the order in which to go through them, should be gone over with the students in the beginning. The stations should also be numbered clearly. In addition, the stations should have clear instructions, either written or illustrated. If students will complete different work at the stations, they can be colour coded.

The role of the teacher during station work is to help students at the stations. This method lets the teacher focus on directing and supporting the lowest achieving students. The benefit of this method is the ability to use peer support. Students can be grouped according to many factors, and they should be varied periodically, according to the principles of differentiation. Pairs and groups can be formed so that there is always one talented student in a group to support a lower achieving peer. Alternatively, students can be grouped based on skill level, so all low-achieving students are in the same group. The students' experience of station work is usually positive. Well-thought out stations keep students interested and focused, and in the best case scenario, the students can practice and review things that they have already learned in the form of a game. Thus, station work is very practical for revising content that has already been learned. Often, stations can be repeated with small changes later on.

We have used station work a lot, for example when teaching foreign languages. For example, it is an effective method for recapping what has been learned. For example, for the duration of one lesson, one can place seven or eight different stations in the classroom. With that arrangement, the working time in each station is quite short. Students can go around the stations in pairs or small groups, based on the number of students. One can have stations that are quite similar, but with slightly different content. For example, one can have handwritten questions or problems at two different stations, or if there are many computers in the classroom, there can be many stations where the students need to use a computer. It is good to think about the different ways to differentiate within single stations. For example, at a conversation station, one can give students prescribed model conversation, and there can be multiple levels of work at stations with handwritten work. Other ways to differentiate foreign language classes can be found in Chapter 10 of this book.

EXAMPLE STATIONS FOR A FOREIGN LANGUAGE LESSON

Differentiation can be done in a lesson by teaching method (station work) or by the contents of the stations. One can also differentiate the group composition by grouping skill levels together, or by mixing different learning profiles.

– Reading and translating the textbook in pairs or groups – one can differentiate by using simplified texts.

– Review questions from the book or worksheet – differentiate by individualised worksheets.

– ICT station, at which online activities are used to review content– differentiate by assigning different levels of online activities.

– Memory game station, at which there are vocabulary words in English or as pictures, along with their counterparts in the foreign language – work method differentiates itself.

– Questioning the partner or group mates about vocabulary words – work method differentiates itself.

– Charades, Pictionary or Taboo station, where vocabulary words are acted out, drawn or explained – work method differentiates itself.

– Conversation station, at which there are verbal activities based on the vocabulary and content learned – work method differentiates itself, but prescribed model conversations can be used.

PROJECTS

Different kinds of projects are well-suited for differentiated instruction. Using them, it is easy to practice things that are important in today's education, such as critical information seeking and widely familiarising oneself with a topic. Projects are especially good for subjects such as history of geography.

In project work, differentiation should start already from choosing the topic. An individualised and personally chosen topic makes the student committed and motivated to complete the work. Before starting the work, one should individually go through the objectives of the project so that each student can have their say in what they think their goal should be. The teacher should also keep in mind that all students' goals do not have to be the same or as wide as their peers'.

Project work itself can be differentiated in many ways. The starting idea should be that all students do not have to produce a similar product according to similar objectives. It is good to give students like Catherine more freedom, so that they can plan the product themselves, as well as come up with how to document the process. Even in information seeking, work can be differentiated by either giving students freedom to research information about their topic, or by offering them more challenging sources from the get-go. For many lower achieving student, this kind of freedom and abstract approach can be difficult. It can be hard for them to progress with their work, if they do not know exactly what to do. These students should be given some guidelines or options to direct their work. In their project, they can stay at surface level with their topic.

Students can also be given example questions to help with information seeking. For instance, if the topic of a science project is bears, helpful questions can include 'What does a bear eat?', 'How and where does a bear live?' or 'What do bears do during winter?'. One can also give prescribed sentence starters or a source to the student, so they can find information more easily. The source can be a textbook or even a specific web page. One should also think about the documentation and end product of the project. A low-achieving student can make a voice recording of their topic and present it with illustrations.

An integral part of differentiated project work is time management. Some students can spend hours on their project, while some only need a shorter amount of time to complete their work to the same level. Differentiating time management can be approached individually, based on the motivation and capacity of the student.

It can also be justified to differentiate the presentations of the end products of the project, especially if one of the students is selectively mute or terrified of performing in front of the class. All students do not have to present their project in front of the class. Instead of this, some students can have a poster station, where the other students can go read their posters in small groups.

When grading project work, it is important to remember the individual objectives of the students. This should be also kept in mind when the students self-evaluate. For one of them, assessment can be focused on information, for another, on the work methods they used, and for a third student, on their behaviour during the project. It is not always necessary for the students to complete a self-evaluation at all, and it can only be done by certain students who benefit from it.

In conclusion, different teaching methods are highlighted in differentiated instruction. In this chapter, we explored some practical teaching methods. However, it is important to approach all teaching according to the principles of differentiation, which were presented in the beginning of the chapter.

Differentiating project work

Beginning

- Let students choose their topic freely. Offer low-achievers some prescribed options.
- Help low-achievers to get started by specifying the topic and the end product.
- With the students, set goals for the project. Individualise objectives if needed.

Work

- Focus on directing low-achievers in working and information seeking.
- Give high-achievers free rein in choosing the product and information seeking.
- Utilise different learning environments, such as different parts of the classroom, corridor and school yard.
- Differentiate the product based on the student's skills. Some students can draw and write a poster; some can make a recording, video or a PowerPoint presentation.
- Differentiate the time taken on the project.

Assessment

- Give a chance to present the product to the class.
- Give a chance to let the other students take a look at one student's poster without putting the student on the spot.
- Differentiate also in self-evaluation.
- Assess projects based on individual objectives.

Tips to remedy the starting point

GRADE 1: SAM

- Alternate different teaching methods and use a functional working approach.
- Give clear and personal instructions. Use pictures for support.
- Shorten the teaching sessions.
- Try to use incentives.
- Seat in the back of the classroom and give permission to move.

GRADE 3: RASMUS

- Try to use incentives.
- Let Rasmus work independently.
- In group work, focus on grouping so that Rasmus only works with a single partner at first.
- Limit the number of tasks to complete.
- Have contractual project workdays and differentiate the workload and quality of the work.

GRADE 5: AMY

- Give remedial education either pro-actively or reactively.
- Try co-teaching with a colleague.
- Teach practical study skills.
- Differentiate the amount and content of tasks.
- Give more time to work.
- Use group work and peer support.
- Differentiate homework.
- Give clear instructions and support them with pictures.

GRADE 9: CATHERINE

- Differentiate tasks by asking for justification or critical consideration for her answers.
- Use materials from higher grade levels, such as upper secondary school.
- Teach self-direction.
- Personalise homework and assign more challenging tasks.
- Guide into different in-depth projects.
- Use Catherine as a peer tutor from time to time.

6. SUPPORT MATERIALS

Starting point

GRADE 1: SAM

Sam gets distracted even by the smallest sound or movement, even though the classroom is generally quiet. Sitting still is hard for Sam, and he leaves his seat easily to bother others. Sam often loses his things and there are chewed-up bits of pencil at the bottom of his backpack. The teacher often directs Sam into the hallway to calm down in the middle of the lesson.

GRADE 3: RASMUS

Independent, handwritten work in his own seat is hard for Rasmus. He gets especially anxious if there is a lot of time to spend working, and often refuses to do his work during lessons. Because of this, Rasmus gets a lot of homework and has to stay indoors during breaks to complete his work.

GRADE 5: AMY

The challenge for Amy are the texts and questions in textbooks. Because of her dyslexia, reading long texts is difficult. Texts are often too complicated in books, and the font is too small. While reading, Amy skips a line often, losing where she was in the text. Amy tries hard to study for tests, but since reading textbooks is hard, she finds this time-consuming and cannot remember anything about what she read.

GRADE 9: CATHERINE

For Catherine, things taught at school are easy, and she would like to delve deeper into history or geography contents. Sometimes Catherine has tried to research more with her phone, but has been told off by the teacher. Catherine has sometimes asked teachers if she can go ahead of the class in the workbook, but they have not allowed it. This is why Catherine usually settles to doodling in her notebook, waiting for the class to end.

In addition to practices shown in previous chapters, teaching can be differentiated using practical equipment and supportive materials. In this chapter, we will look at the penultimate section of the 5D model: supportive material, and its differentiated and flexible use. The chapter is divided into two themes, which are *the differentiated use of teaching tools and learning materials,* and *the tools for concentration.* We have already touched on learning materials in Chapter 5, but in this context, we will focus on it from a practical standpoint. Differentiation of different subjects is explored in Part IV of the book.

THE DIFFERENTIATED USE OF TEACHING TOOLS AND LEARNING MATERIALS

Some series of textbooks nowadays offer specialised material for low-achieving students, which, in essence, is a good thing. Usually, in these tasks and texts have been simplified to focus on the core content of the teaching. This kind of material is well-suited for some students. However, the problem of readily prepared materials is the same as mainstream textbooks. They only offer one level of material for a single type of student. Unfortunately, application activities have often been completely cut out of such materials. Furthermore, sometimes special material does not differ much from the mainstream, which does not help low-achieving students. Special materials are also often a lot more expensive, which is difficult for most schools to accommodate in their budgets. Although a good addition to one's tool kit, no equipment or pre-differentiated learning material alone is enough to replace the differentiation of teaching as a whole. All equipment and materials need to be individually assessed from the perspective of the student's needs.

IMAGE 4. Teaching support material should be used flexibly and individually

ACQUIRING LEARNING MATERIALS

One should start by assessing the needs of the student when acquiring new learning materials. There are some learning materials and educational equipment out there for differentiated teaching of lowest achieving students. When buying materials, one should focus especially on whether the material can be used in different ways. Teaching materials and visual aids from the lower grade levels can work well for low achieving students, for example with a student like Amy. In addition to the level of the students, the age of the students poses a challenge for learning materials. With older students, the material from lower grade levels is too childish, and thus, demotivating. Amy does not get excited about the texts and content that one can still use for younger students.

One can look for differentiating materials for one's low-achieving students from companies and publishing houses who specialise in learning materials, but also from websites of organisations who focus on specialised support in education. For example, some associations may sell supporting tools for students with dyslexia, and if necessary, offers education in how to use those tools at a reasonable price. Sometimes the same product can be much more expensive in a specialist shop than in a mainstream one. For example, a triangle support to help grip the pencil correctly can be bought from a stationary shop for much less than going to a specialised education-related shop.

Many schools have active parents' associations which are willing to support the school and the students. If the budget is tight, the support of the parents' association is valuable. Parents' associations can also make rapid decisions and purchases, because often they are not bound by such restrictions as having to request several quotations for a single purchase. Sometimes independent companies in the region are also willing to support the local schools by donating specific materials.

Out of principle, we do not recommend spending your own money to buy learning materials. We believe that an employer should always pay for equipment used at work. However, since we know that many teachers buy materials with their own money, we would like to remind you, that in some countries, professional equipment and literature – such as this book – are eligible to be deducted from taxes.

Tips for acquiring learning materials and equipment

- Remember to find material that can be used in multiple ways.
- Remember different places for acquiring materials – organisations, publishing houses and book shops.
- Use materials from the lower grades at higher grade level.
- Remember that one does not always have to buy materials. There are plenty of free materials available for differentiation, such as texts in plain language.

COMBINE, PRODUCE AND SHARE MATERIALS

Differentiating instruction does not necessarily require the school to invest in equipment or materials. Often, the same materials and equipment a teacher uses for visual aids otherwise in their work are the best tools to differentiate teaching. Even for the students, having familiar tools makes the threshold lower for using them. If the teacher has been using certain manipulatives with Sam's class to visualise mathematics, Sam can find it easier to use them to support his own calculations, too.

Often, the teacher should first edit the material to suit their students, even from the point of view of learning results. Above all, differentiation requires changing the way the teaching and learning material available is used. Along with pre-differentiated materials, one should mix and match ideas from different book series and utilise lower grade levels' materials.

In differentiation, especially making materials is found particularly troublesome. We recommend starting a communal material bank on a cloud file or book shelf in the teachers' lounge at school. The benefit of electronic materials is that one can easily edit it to match the needs of the students. Thus, the material teachers make by themselves is often the best suited for teaching. With the common material bank, the most important thing is clearly cataloguing it by subject and topic. A good template for this are the table of contents pages of textbooks that are used at school. Then, prepared material can easily be found at any given time, even years after. One should start collecting and sharing materials even alone, since it lowers the threshold for others to follow suit and share their own creations.

When making differentiated material, one should remember websites from which one can find a lot of teaching materials for different subjects. Many sites share materials for free, for example in mathematics. In addition, teachers have many groups on social media, in which they share ideas and materials for differentiation. When you create good materials, you should share it. When the open culture spreads, one can find new materials more easily.

REMEMBER CLARITY IN MATERIALS

Especially on higher grade levels, texts in humanities and sciences are often too difficult for students with dyslexia, like Amy. These texts can also be too long and complex for immigrant students. Students like these would benefit from texts with simpler vocabulary and grammatical structures. It has been estimated that 8-12% of children and youth in Finland would need plain language texts (Virtanen 2014). Many students can finish their school with mainstream texts, but this may not lead to optimal learning results. Even we as adults could think which one we would have an easier time to find information from, a 20-page scientific article or a summary in plain language. All texts do not have to be made from the start. Materials are readily available in plain language. For example, in many countries, one can often find a version of the news in plain language.

In some textbook series, shorter and simplified chapters can be available as extra material, and as such, should be used with low-achievers. Of course, these are only appropriate for students at a specific skill level. Sometimes, there may be a student in the class who would benefit from only short summaries, a few sentences long. One can also offer a plain text version alongside the regular text, so they can be used for test revision, for example. It is also good to remember that the purpose of differentiation is not to make studying too easy, but to enable everyone's studying in their zone of proximal development (see Chapter 1). Thus, even plain texts should not be too easy for the student. Once again, the vital knowledge of one's students is highlighted.

Often, teachers feel that they do not have time to create texts in plain language. You could occasionally enlist the help of high-achievers in this. This differentiates in itself and saves the teacher's time. For example, one can give Catherine a task to read a text and write a short summary of it. This can be a reading comprehension exercise in first language classes, since this works towards objectives in first language subjects. The material produced by the high-achiever can later serve as learning material for a lower achiever. A high-achiever can also take a text and create a little vocabulary from it in foreign language class. The student can send these to the teacher by email, so that the teacher can have them available, and edit them according to students' needs later. For example, the teacher can replace some words in the vocabulary if needed, add highlights or underlines, or even separate syllables for students who have a hard time reading. Alternatively, one can instruct a learning assistant to make each student a little booklet of history texts in plain language and bigger font size. This way, the teacher does not have to do everything themselves.

Often, a student with dyslexia is challenged by the small font size in a textbook, as well as reading long words without the syllables separated. In plain language texts, it is important to make sure the font size is big enough, as well as to keep the spaces between words and rows big enough, to make it easier for the student to comprehend the text. One can easily make text bigger by photocopying texts and magnifying them onto a bigger page. This way, texts are easier to annotate, underline and highlight. A child who is learning to read, or a student like Amy who has a hard time reading and remembering texts, can benefit from marking syllables in one word with a different colour.

One can also make reading regular texts easier. A student with dyslexia can use a magnifying glass to make sense of small text, or perhaps tinted plastic sheets to put over the page, since a background colour can sometimes make reading easier. The magnifying glass can be carried in the pencil case, and the colour sheet can be in the backpack, so that they are always available for the student to use, even at home. Sometimes the texts can even be printed on coloured paper, if this helps the student decipher text better. Before a school culture that embraces differentiation has been established, the texts can be printed on coloured paper for all students, even though it is meant to only support one student's learning. With smaller students, who have difficulties in visual perception, so-called 'reading windows' are often useful, as they highlight a certain word of the text. A reading ruler can also be used with older students.

GATHER A WIDE VARIETY OF TEACHING TOOLS AND VISUAL AIDS IN THE CLASSROOM

It is beneficial for differentiation if the physical learning environment is full of stimulating and pedagogical material that is accessible to the students during the school day. It is good for the material to have its own place, perhaps in the back of the classroom. Different counting tools, such as blocks and fraction 'pies', can be in a basket on a shelf, from where the students can get them to help them with calculations. In a languages classroom, there can also be a place for literature in foreign languages, such as books and magazines. This kind of supportive material can be acquired from homes as a donation, in order to not use school funds.

It is also beneficial to have as many pedagogical teaching games as possible in the classroom. Even classic board games can be used in differentiation. They teach foreign languages, counting, adhering to rules and group work. For example, chess is linked to developing the student's mathematical thinking. Playing can improve group spirit and act as a reward for older students, whom stickers and stamps do not motivate anymore. One can consciously direct a low-achiever to play certain kinds of games, which develop specifically those areas the student finds challenging. In an ideal situation, the student practices and improves the skills they find difficult through a game. One can differentiate the learning of Sam and Rasmus, both of whom have a hard time working for a long time, by letting them play a certain game towards the end of the lesson. A student can also be motivated by giving them a whole game lesson, if school life has gone well for a set period of time. In addition, a student struggling with homework can play a certain game in the evenings, for example for a week, which will motivate the student more than mainstream homework. One should not undermine the importance of games, even with older students. One can also ask the homes, whether they have any old games that can be used with students.

ADVISE AND INSTRUCT IN USING THE MATERIAL

The use of support materials in differentiation requires learning from both the teacher and the student. For the student, the challenge cannot only be acknowledging and accepting the need for the materials or equipment, but also the way the equipment is used. Acknowledging and accepting the need for the equipment is helped by the working culture in which the different needs and objectives are verbalised openly (see Chapter 4). However, one should teach the use of supporting materials age-appropriately. The goal is the self-direction of the students. One can direct the student by saying: 'How would you depict this calculation with blocks? Go get them' or 'Would the tools in the math box help with this one?'.

One should spend a lot of time teaching independent use of differentiating equipment and supporting materials. The student should be taught to get and use the material and equipment, as well as putting it all back in place after the work is done. In the beginning, one should get familiar with the new materials with the whole group, and they can be accessible to everyone. When the novelty wears off, the material is dropped by those who do not really need it. However, supporting material and equipment, such as fraction pies in mathematics, are especially well-suited for teaching the basics to the whole group. When the equipment is readily available, their use will continue with those students who need the support. One can verbalise the usefulness of the materials and equipment out loud: 'Did you notice how this helped you focus on the task better?' 'Using the fraction pies, you figured out this problem so well!'

UTILISE INFORMATION TECHNOLOGY

One can also use different ICT equipment and solutions in differentiation. Nowadays, there are many different levels of online activities that can be used to differentiate mathematics and languages. Computer-based activities can also help to motivate the student. The student can spend a part of the lesson on the computer, and one can also assign those tasks as homework. Many web systems can save the game, so that the game can be continued where it was left off. In addition, some programmes let the teacher monitor the students and their progress. For example, there are many of these applications for reading and spelling. Some games also change based on the skill level of the student, which makes them good for differentiation for both low and high-achievers. For example, one can direct a student like Catherine to play a challenging game either on a computer or a tablet.

When considering tools for differentiation, one should keep the objective of the teaching in mind. If the student has challenges with the fine motor skills of their hand, it is justified to let them use a computer or tablet while writing, alongside a triangle support for a pencil. Computers and tablets also serve children with dyslexia, since one can easily zoom into text using those. In addition, many word-processing programmes correct spelling mistakes and mark them with red, which improves spelling accuracy. One could let Rasmus, who hates writing by hand, to do his work on the computer sometimes, if it makes him work considerably better.

Some programmes convert speech into text, which makes them good for low-achievers to use for taking notes. Alternatively, a weak writer can record their voice to take notes. One can give the student a recording device, or they can simply use their phone. Phones can be used in teaching in many ways. They can be used to take pictures of what the teacher writes on the board, translate words in foreign language class or look up information and events in history. At home, one can record verbal answers to questions in homework, thus avoiding writing. Once again, we encourage you to be creative and think about the individual needs of the student. The older the students are, the more reason there is to listen to their perspective.

Audiobooks are a noteworthy option for a student like Amy, who has dyslexia. We have had students whose reading has been at word-by-word level in third grade, but who have not had any other issues with learning. In these cases, these students have participated in class, for example in science and religious education, but they have had audiobooks to use. Some book series have the audio versions online.

Sometimes, it is possible to scan the text book to be read or filled-in on a computer. This can be done by the student themselves, or a teacher or learning assistant. In many countries, copyright laws allow for scanning of physical books for individual use, if the reason for it is a disability or illness. According to that, physical books can be scanned for those who cannot use the physical book, for example due to dyslexia. However, we advise you to find out about the relevant legislation in your respective country.

In addition, one can get applications on tablets and computers that read books out loud. One of these is Voice Dream, which is compatible with the iPad. Often, these applications can be used to upload texts from an e-library, or to upload text straight from the internet. On the tablet, one can magnify text, or change its background colour to make perception easier. One can learn to read out loud with the class using a tablet or computer. It is important that, as the computer reads out loud, the student listens to it while following the text themselves, if possible. After the computer reads the text once, the student can also read it independently after. The benefit of machines is that sometimes one can adjust the speed at which they read, based on the level of the student. If there are no electronical equipment available for teaching, texts can also be read and recorded for the student to use at home afterwards.

The flexible use of teaching equipment and supporting materials

- Offer a stimulating learning environment.
- Use plain language texts with low-achievers.
- Remember material banks online.
- Share the teaching material you make with others.
- Increase the font size for a weak reader and make sure the spaces between words and lines are big enough.
- Illustrate the important parts of text with underlining and highlighting.
- Use coloured sheets, printing on coloured paper, a magnifying glass or a reading window.
- Utilise audiobooks and scan physical books, if needed.
- Use a variety of online activities.
- Utilise the students' own devices, for example with information seeking.
- Try to use a computer to support a student who has a hard time writing.

TOOLS FOR CONCENTRATION

Alongside learning material and teaching equipment, there is a lot of supporting material for schoolwork itself. Loud noise and general commotion bother most students and make focusing more difficult. For some students, even the smallest of sounds, such as an eraser falling on the floor or a chair creaking, can distract their attention from the important things. Especially for students who have a sensory processing disorder, problems in handling sensory information can cause challenges in teaching, as the student can find loud noises very unpleasant. Thus, it is extremely important that there be as much peace for working in the classroom as possible. It is also possible to support the concentration of the students by individual practices, some of which are addressed in what follows.

REDUCE STIMULI

Different auditive stimuli especially affect students like Sam while working in the classroom. The student can then benefit from wearing earmuffs or noise-cancelling headphones while working. For example, in special needs classrooms, in which students often do different things at once, each student can have their own pair of earmuffs or headphones. This way, using them becomes normal. In a mainstream classroom, earmuffs also serve the practice of flexible grouping. While the teacher instructs some students with an activity, other students can focus on their written assignments using earmuffs.

Some students can find big earmuffs or headphones uncomfortable, as they can press hard on their head, or be otherwise unpleasant. A student like this can try ear plugs instead of big headphones. They are easy to keep with you, and they can be flexibly used during a school day. In addition, they are harder to notice, which is why older students might prefer them over bulky headphones. Alternatively, one can let a student listen to music in class, if it helps them focus and does not interfere with studying.

One can reduce visual stimuli in many ways. In Chapter 4, we explored the importance of the learning environment, and highlighted the restrained use of visual materials on the walls, along with considering seating arrangements in the classroom. For example, a student like Sam should not be seated in the middle of the classroom, since he would be surrounded by a lot of visual stimuli. One can reduce the visual stimuli of a single student by partitions. One should have light partitions that can be easily moved in the classroom, based on the situation. For an example, while focusing on something very important, such as a test, a student can temporarily corner oneself off from the rest of the class.

One should create a culture in which students can independently get a light partition while focusing on work. Students themselves often find the use of partitions useful and are happy to use them. Sometimes, especially with younger children, students almost compete for the use of the partitions. Then, the teacher should use their authority and make sure that the partitions go to those who need them the most. Instead of using partitions, one can divide the space with mobile shelving units, or the student can be directed to turn their desk away from others, towards the wall of the classroom, in order to reduce visual stimuli. Alternatively, one can let some students to wear their hood or cap in class, if it specifically helps them with concentrating.

MAKE SITTING STILL EASIER

Many energetic students find it hard to sit still. Especially young students like Sam can easily leave their seat to move around in the classroom. Older children have learned to sit at their desk over the years, but the excess energy manifests as squirminess. The optimal situation would be that the student has an adjustable desk that can be adjusted to suit sitting and standing up. However, very few schools have the money for this. To make this resource available, one could only purchase these desks for students who need it for working properly.

It is important to include active work and exercise in teaching. However, at school, there are situations during which one must sit still. Then, one can try equipment and special support to help a student sit still. For example, seat cushions and pillows can help some students to work at a desk. Sometimes, one can also try a completely different chair. For example, using an exercise ball as a seat can work for some students, since this allows small movement. Some also benefit from an office chair that can swivel or spin.

Hyperactivity can also manifest as excessive movement of the feet and legs, which should be allowed. However, sometimes this can distract the student from their own work, or at its worst, bother other students, if the student kicks their classmates. A foam roll often used in physio therapy can be used in this case, as the student can roll their feet on it. Alternatively, one can have a balance board under the desk, on which the student can rest their feet and move them in a controlled way. This could be made by one of the high-achievers in woodwork class as an extra credit project. Another useful trick is to put big rubber band around the legs of the desk, which the student can move with their feet.

Sometimes hyperactive children like Sam use a weight vest to make sitting and focusing easier. One can also use a weighted plush toy for this. The idea is to have this weight across the student's thighs, where it relaxes them and makes it easier to work and concentrate. One can tell the student that the stuffed animal only likes to sit on someone's lap, so they naturally use this tool correctly. In a classroom of small children, this toy often becomes an important mascot that gets a name.

SUPPORT INDEPENDENT WORK

All teachers know students who easily break their pencils and crumple their notebooks. The student does not always do this maliciously, since some find it hard to focus while not fiddling with something. The students can then be given a small object, such as a small bean bag, stress ball, play dough or even blu tack. Small students can even bring a small plush toy from home to fiddle with during class. Alternatively, a student can be allowed to draw in their book while the teacher talks. It is important to direct the student to channel their energy in an appropriate way, so that school equipment stays intact. One should test supporting equipment in practice to make sure they are beneficial, and get rid of them if they do not work. However, sometimes these supporting equipment can become very popular. This happened with fidget spinners and fidget cubes, which became very popular among all students in Finland in 2017, so much so that they became a nuisance.

Some students' pencils, erasers and even sleeves are full of teeth marks. For some students, this is merely a habit, for others it is a symptom of sensory integration difficulties. There are also some students who find that chewing on something helps with concentrating on listening and working. These students can be allowed to chew gum in class, if it helps them focus and keeps equipment and clothes intact. Nowadays, there are chew toys available for this purpose, which can be used with younger students. The chew toy is made of a safe material and can hang from a student's neck or wrist. This way, it is always with the student and they can chew on it during class to help them focus.

Structuring work and dividing it into smaller sections can be helpful for a student struggling with an attention deficit. A test, or another long piece of work, can be broken down so that each part is on a separate sheet of paper. The student can then pick up the next sheet from a prescribed place, after finishing the first one. The student can also be instructed to periodically sharpen their pencil in a prescribed area in the classroom. This allows for natural movement in the classroom, even during a long piece of work or independent study. One can also print different activities on different coloured papers. This makes it easier for the student to see the transition from one task to another.

One can use an hourglass to demonstrate the time spent on work. With Sam or Rasmus, one could have a practice in which the student will work until the hourglass is empty. After this, they get a little break of the same duration. This kind of a compromise is often surprisingly beneficial, and many students learn this method quickly and become independent in using it. Using an hourglass motivates the students to work actively, as many students get satisfaction from competing against themselves, for example to find out how many mathematics problems they can solve during the time it takes for the sand in the hourglass to empty entirely from the top chamber into the bottom. One can also demonstrate the passing of time by using the time timer clock we already mentioned in the previous chapter. The time timer clock shows the time meant to be spent working with the colour red, which gets smaller and smaller as time passes. Time timer clocks can be bought as large versions, so that they can be used with the whole class. Smaller time timers are suitable for single students. One can also use a phone timer or even an egg timer.

Different ways to support concentration

- Earmuffs, ear plugs or listening to music with headphones
- Wearing a hood or a cap
- Partitions
- Seating cushions, exercise balls or special chairs
- Things to fiddle with, such as blu tack, a stress ball or a bean bag
- Allowing the student to draw
- Structuring work, an hourglass, a time timer clock or an egg timer

In conclusion, let it be noted that one can support learning with many different kinds of equipment. In this chapter, we only highlighted a few examples. One should share good experiences, since many teachers grapple with similar challenges. In addition, occupational therapists can give good practical tips regarding support for the students' work and concentration. It is good to remind you that the equipment is not the actual purpose, but they are only meant to make some challenges at school easier to handle. Thus, it does not matter whether the student benefits from a specialist stress toy or a bean bag from the school gym. Similarly, instead of a professional seat cushion, the student can bring a pillow from home, if it works well for them. We encourage you to test different and innovative solutions.

Differentiation practices are very individualised; a piece of equipment that works for one student can do nothing at all for another. In some cases, that specific equipment can even bother some students. For example, Sam could benefit from drawing or fiddling with blu tack, but this could distract Amy a lot. One should test different solutions and assess the benefit for each approach with the student and, if needed, the parents. The most important thing is that one has a natural attitude towards the use of supporting equipment, which is, again, related to a school culture that accepts difference.

One should talk openly about supporting material and equipment in class, which makes the students less ashamed for needing the support. For example, wearing glasses can serve as a good example to explain how some students need special equipment in the classroom. In the school community, all teaching equipment and differentiating material should be flexibly available to the whole school. Sometimes, teachers can have materials in their cupboards that their students have used in the past. Supporting equipment should have their own place in a communal storage cupboard in the school. This way, all teachers can use them, if necessary.

Tips to remedy the starting point

GRADE 1: SAM

- Reduce visual and auditory stimuli by using partitions and/or earmuffs.
- Try a seat cushion, a weight plush, or a foam roll to support sitting still.
- Allow a stress ball, bean bag or play dough to support concentration.
- Use electronic educational games for motivation.

GRADE 3: RASMUS

- Demonstrate the time spent on work with a time timer or an hourglass.
- Utilise electronic games.
- Let Rasmus answer questions in the workbook by computer sometimes.
- Try motivating him with different supporting materials, such as a magnifying glass or coloured sheets.

GRADE 5: AMY

- Utilise plain language texts, coloured sheets, a magnifying glass or a reading window.
- Scan books if necessary, and offer audiobooks in different subjects.
- Teach to utilise IT in studying, for example by taking notes by recording or using a picture of writing on the board.
- Offer practical tools to support different subjects (see Part IV).

GRADE 9: CATHERINE

- Utilise e-learning materials and educational games from different grade levels.
- Direct to familiarise herself deeper with the content, for example by using a phone or tablet.
- Differentiate the end of the class by asking Catherine to make a summary of the chapter by computer.

7. ASSESSMENT

The starting point

GRADE 1: SAM

Sam has a strong, albeit unrealistic, perception of himself as a learner. He also cannot handle disappointment very well. Often, Sam disagrees with the teacher about assessment, and he finds it hard to accept negative feedback. Sam expects a perfect performance from himself, and gets disappointed when he usually cannot reach this. The disappointment manifests itself as negative behaviour at school.

GRADE 3: RASMUS

Rasmus does not particularly care about assessment or the feedback of the teacher. Assessment does not seem to have any impact on his learning. For example, Rasmus does not see the connection between test grades and his own learning.

GRADE 5: AMY

Amy gets nervous about tests. She studies a lot for them, but cannot show her knowledge in them, as she underachieves constantly. Amy gets bad grades from tests, which is reflected on her perception of herself as a learner.

GRADE 9: CATHERINE

Catherine gets full marks from tests. Her report cards are all straight A's. Catherine completes given tasks well, but does not independently strive for any higher goals.

In this chapter, we will discuss the last dimension in our 5D model, which is assessment from the viewpoint of differentiation. Assessment is a topic that teachers talk about a lot, and one that puzzles and even divides teachers. Simultaneously, teachers still take assessment seriously, as it is seen as one of the most important parts of education. In this book, we do not strive to extensively define assessment or its purposes. Instead, this book highlights the *differentiation* and *practice of assessment*. However, in order for everyone to understand the differentiation of assessment in the same way, we will begin with a short exploration into *common principles, forms* and *objectives of assessment.*

COMMON PRINCIPLES OF ASSESSMENT

Assessment has a broad role and means different things to different people. For a teacher, assessment gives information about the student's progress and helps with planning and practising instruction. For a student, it speaks of learning results and changes the student's perception of themselves as a learner. Simultaneously, assessment supports the common pedagogical relationship between the school and the home, by giving parents information about the student's situation and learning. Assessment is also societally important, as it directs students into further studies and gives national information about the effectiveness of education. Because of these reasons, assessment is important for the due process of the teacher and student alike. For example, assessment given to students in higher grade levels has a direct effect on their future opportunities in higher education. For the teacher, assessment is evidence and confirmation about the content learned in class, as the assessments are directly related to content and objectives that the students learn.

Assessment directs schoolwork and learning more than any other factor (Hayward 2012; Hodgson & Pang 2012). Due to this, it is important to focus one's assessment on the correct things. If only certain specific content is emphasised in assessment, instead of large, contextualised concepts, it is clear that specific trivia knowledge is highlighted in teaching as well. This phenomenon can be seen in education cultures in countries that put a lot of emphasis on assessment and testing. The things that are measured by assessment are those things that are emphasised in teaching. At its worst, this can lead into education being rendered into mere preparation for tests and the content learned becomes simply tricks to do well in assessments. In countries like Finland, where the curriculum emphasises transversal competence, the assessment also focuses on wider goals.

For parents, the most visible form of assessment is the feedback that is brought home, along with evidence of the student's skills. Although assessment is a much wider concept for us teachers than single grades or performances, we have noticed that, in practice, some teachers assess learning in a rather narrow manner. In this narrow assessment practice, test grades are highlighted too much, at the expense of holistic exhibition of skills. Although testing is an easy, uniform way of assessment for all teachers, it does not traditionally consider the different needs of students, and thus, give a realistic picture of the students' capabilities or progress.

Overall, assessment should be not only individualised, but also equitable and reasonable. For example, Sam and Rasmus, who often disrupt teaching, occasionally get worse grades in certain subjects than they would actually deserve. However, assessment should be focused on specifically those objectives that have been set for each student. The actions due to problems with behaviour or attention should not be considered in assessment of content learning. We have compiled some important aspects about assessments in Figure 10.

ASSESSMENT SHOULD NOT BE:
- only numerical and non-descriptive
- comparing a student with other students' performance
- only looking backwards
- negative and hard to understand
- revolving around the personality of the student
- based on anything outside learning objectives

INSTEAD, ASSESSMENT SHOULD BE:
- both descriptive and numerical
- focused on the student's own learning process
- guiding the learner forward
- constructive and easy to understand
- based on learning objectives
- individualised, planned and encouraging in active learning

FIGURE 10. The integral aspects of assessment from the perspective of differentiation

THE DIFFERENT FORMS OF ASSESSMENT AND THEIR OBJECTIVES

Assessment is not some detached part of education, but should be constant and consistent. Thus, one should assess learning every day while teaching. Students often make the connection between the word 'assessment' and a written test that comes at the end of term. Often, even at home, assessment is conflated with a test grade or the report card. However, these are only one form of assessment, called summative assessment. Assessment can be roughly divided into three forms: *pre-assessment, formative assessment* and *summative assessment*. In teaching, one should practice each of these. There are many ways to practice them, and one can always come up with new ways. When picking a method for practising them, it is important to consider whether it will give you the necessary information for assessment.

PRE-ASSESSMENT. When the purpose of assessment is to see what the student knows and how the student learns before the content is taught, this is called pre-assessment. Sometimes this is also referred to as diagnostic assessment. The purpose of pre-assessment is to figure out what the student knows and can do, in order to tailor teaching according to their needs. For example, with a new class, or a new student joining a pre-existing class, the teacher should carefully become familiar with their background and potential transcripts. In addition, for example in mathematics or language and literature, one can hold a baseline test to find out what the student's initial skills are. This directs instruction and its differentiation. Pre-assessment can also be used as an aid to differentiation, for example when planning teaching groups. Pre-assessment also helps the student to connect what they already know with what they are about to learn.

FORMATIVE ASSESSMENT. When assessment happens during the work and is focused on the learning process, this is formative assessment. The most important thing in formative assessment is constant and consistent feedback. It is meant to monitor the progress of learning, and thus enable the direction of the learning process of a single student or the whole group. In this context, we would like to bring up self-assessment, which is a very important part of formative assessment, and which is unfortunately often only practiced retrospectively. From the perspective of differentiation, formative assessment is meaningful because it helps teachers recognise how instruction should be differentiated for each student. Formative assessment also includes the constant verbalisation of differentiation, as it makes the progress of the student more visible.

In addition to self-assessment, based on the age and development level of the students, formative assessment methods can include different checklists, learning journals or other reflection on learning. It is good to note that none of this has to be done in writing, and many of these can be completed using different learning platforms. For example, Rasmus' learning can be directed by giving him a checklist, from which he can make sure that he completes the steps of a project in the correct order. The learning of younger students can be monitored by considering their answers and questions. Even small children can be directed to check their own work independently and to make their learning apparent to the teacher, and to themselves, using self-assessment.

SUMMATIVE ASSESSMENT. When the knowledge of a student is assessed in the end of a period of study, we talk about summative assessment. Summative assessment should make visible what the student has learned, and it must consist of learning objectives, content and teaching methods. Even summative assessment does not have to be written. Summative assessment can also be made in a group or individually. While the rest of the class does the written assessment, Amy can show her knowledge verbally with the teacher or learning assistant. She can even video herself talking about the content with her phone. The most important thing is that the end product showcases the student's capability. More specific assessment methods are explored later in this chapter, along with the differentiation of those methods.

DIFFERENTIATED ASSESSMENT

In Finland differentiation is a pre-requirement for all assessment. The Finnish National Core Curriculum for Basic Education states the following:

> *Versatile assessment methods shall be used. The teacher gathers information on the pupils' progress in various areas of learning and in different learning situations. In this context, it is important to take into account the pupils' different ways of learning and work approaches and to ensure that there are no obstacles to demonstrating progress and achievement. In various assessment and demonstration situations, it is ensured that each pupil understands the assignment and has enough time to complete it. The possibilities of using information and communication technology and giving oral demonstrations of knowledge and skills are also ensured where necessary. Additionally, the accessibility of any aids that the pupils may need is ensured, and the required assistant services are provided. Even mild learning difficulties and any shortcomings in the pupils' skills in the language of instruction [...] should be taken into account when planning and implementing assessment and demonstration situations.* (FNCCBE 2014, section 6.2).

As it states, versatile assessment does, by nature, support differentiation. Good assessment emphasises more the goals than the content of learning. Therefore, a teacher needs to always keep in mind what and why he/she is assessing and what is the fundamental goal of the teaching. Too often assessment in the classroom focuses on superficial and irrelevant pieces of information rather that the holistic view, which in-holds also the student's activity and the overall understanding of the studied phenomenon.

From the perspective of the learning process, the student should know what is being assessed. Is the assessment based on one test or product, working habits or learning content? A student like Catherine is used to getting full marks on a test. If the objective of the assessment is not clear, the grade can be confusing for the student and the parents. Getting full marks in a test does not necessarily mean one has hit all learning objectives. One should consistently involve students in setting and monitoring the learning objectives. If the objective is only mentioned once in the beginning of the year, it is clear that the student will no longer remember it come Christmas. This type of goal-setting does not serve the learning process in any way.

For example, Rasmus and Sam have clearly unrealistic perspectives of themselves as learners. By involving the students in setting the learning objectives, the teacher can guide the assessment process in the right direction even before the assessment is happening. This helps Rasmus and Sam understand and utilise their strengths. According to the students' age level, you can make a list, picture, chart or map about the things you have set to learn together. When the teacher observes a new skill or goal, the student can mark that as achieved. The student can be asked to set goals for themselves outside of school. However, these goals must be monitorable at school. These goals could be learning to ride a bike, or even going to sleep at a certain time. Verbalising these goals improves the student's self-knowledge and it lets the student practice setting personal goals.

Positive feedback is very important in assessment. This is highlighted with low-achievers in particular because those students do not often get positive feedback for their work. Feedback directs our perception of ourselves as learners, and thus has a direct effect on learning results. When giving feedback, it is important to emphasise and uplift the strengths and reached goals of the students. It should be remembered that strengths can also be qualities that are often overlooked in traditional school learning, such as persistence, innovativeness, trying hard, sense of humour, sense of justice, being encouraging and empathy. While assessing the student's work, teachers can say one thing in multiple ways. Teachers should consider how to put things, so that the student will understand the meaning of the feedback correctly. Sometimes we, as teachers, understand things wrong. Is the student who is slow to complete their work truly slow, or simply pensive? Is a student unyielding or assertive during group work?

In previous chapters, we have written a lot about the importance of school culture in differentiation. The same goes with assessment. Assessment culture develops in the school only when discussions on assessments occur more often by teachers and students. From the perspective of differentiated assessment, transparency, openness and fairness are highlighted. It is good to verbalise the practices of differentiated assessment. For example, extra time on a test should not be a secret between Amy and her teacher, but should be available to all students if they find it necessary.

Assessment from the perspective of differentiation

- Go through the objectives, contents and forms of assessment of the period of study with the student.
- Make sure that the student understands what, how and why they are assessed.
- Differentiate assessment practices according to each student. Let them show their skills in a way that suits them.
- Remember versatile and multifaceted assessment.
- Have the student take part in setting goals, the learning process and the method of assessment. Remember that the student is the expert in their own actions, even when they cannot verbalise the reasons behind their actions.
- Give positive feedback and highlight the student's strengths whenever possible.
- Handle negative feedback directly, but constructively.
- Remember the transparency and openness of assessment.
- Remember to be clear and to make sure you are understood.

DIFFERENTIATED ASSESSMENT IN PRACTICE

Different methods of assessment serve different purposes, as we have shown previously. The teacher should remind themselves what, how and, especially, why they assess the students at a given time. In terms of differentiated instruction, it is important that the student understands what is assessed and that the student has a say in the method of assessment. Next, we will explore some of the most common assessment methods from the perspective of differentiation.

SELF AND PEER ASSESSMENT. In self-assessment, the student's own activity and ownership over the learning process are highlighted. These are integral aspects of learning. However, unfortunately often, these vital parts of education are outsourced and the student is left to wait for feedback for their knowledge and skills. In self-assessment, the role of the student in their own learning is enhanced. The student has to think about important questions regarding their own education: What kind of a learner am I? How do I learn best? Simultaneously, the student becomes aware of their own objectives. Self-assessment should be practiced with the students in a smaller scale constantly, as well as at the end of every period of study in a larger scale. Often, self-assessment is conducted only as a short questionnaire at the end of a period of study. However, constant self-assessment and the participation of students in assigning their learning goals with the teacher are very important in terms of the learning process.

Self-assessment can also be differentiated. Some students are good at reflecting on their own learning. They can understand their own learning objectives and how to reach them. Some need more help with this. For example, one can practice self- assessment with students like Rasmus and Sam every day. It does not have to be a large-scale assessment. A simple talk with the student will do, in which the student analyses their own learning. One can progress in small steps. At the end of the class, one can ask the student to tell what they learned, what went well, and what they still need to practice. With older students, large-scale written self-assessments can also be differentiated. The highest achievers can freely assess themselves, whereas one can give low-achievers prescribed questions they should answer, or even give the questions in multiple choice form, so they can choose the answers they find most appropriate.

Peer assessment can be a strange thing for many students, and this should be practiced from first grade levels onwards. First, this should be practiced in a small scale in pairs, and later on in small groups. At first, the students can have a ready-made assessment template, on which they mark their answers with a tick. At the next step, the students' task could be to come up with one positive thing about their peer's work. Peer assessment improves the social relationships of the classroom, and thus positively affects the social learning environment. For example, students like Sam or Amy can have a very negative perception of themselves as learners. Thus, getting positive feedback can be very important and motivating for them. It will also help them create a more positive self-perception. For younger students, one can have lists of good qualities they could choose from to describe the work they are assessing.

Self and peer assessment from the perspective of differentiation

- Practice self and peer assessment consistently.
- Consistently involve students in setting their goals.
- One should also differentiate self and peer assessment. The object and method of assessment should be set based on the capabilities of the student.
- Also practice self-assessment verbally.
- Direct peer assessment towards positive feedback.
- Peer assessment should be started in pairs before moving to group assessments.

TESTING. It should be noted that assessment does not require written tests, and those do not have to be done with all students. For example, Amy is clearly anxious about test situations, which makes her underachieve in tests. Because of this, tests can be left out for her. If one wants to have tests for everyone, Amy's test should be heavily differentiated. For example, a written test does not necessarily measure Amy's true capacity, and is not an appropriate method to assess her.

Although assessment can be completely practiced without traditional tests, most teachers are likely to have them. Especially in lower secondary school, the most commonly used method for assessment is testing. Although we want to emphasise the variety in assessment, we do not forbid the use of tests as a means for assessment. Sometimes a test can motivate the student to learn things. One can, and should, practice a test situation. The student should learn to recognise and utilise their strengths also during tests. For example, Amy can practice differentiated test situations, but prove her knowledge additionally with some form of portfolio.

We would like to remind you that a test situation itself is a one-off assessment, and does not in any way fulfil the objective for continuous and consistent assessment. Furthermore, a test situation is very hard for many students, and it does not give a realistic picture of a student's true capabilities. Thus, one should approach testing from the perspective of differentiation. When differentiated, even testing can be a method for formative assessment. For example, in a mathematics test, a student can verbalise the reason why solving the problem the way they do to a teacher or learning assistant.

Even while preparing for a test, one should keep differentiation in mind. Tests should be in-line with the students' goals and with what they have been taught. The test that comes with the textbook does not always fulfil these criteria. The teacher should draft their tests according to the objectives of the curriculum. For example, instead of learning historical dates by heart, a history test can be a reflection on what it would be like to live as a child during a certain period of history, or what historical sources one could use to find information about a certain historical event.

While preparing for tests, students can come up with test questions alone or in groups. Simultaneously, they have to think about what is truly important about the content they have learned. At first, questions are repetitive, but when directed, the students learn to ask the vital questions about the content. Test questions the students come up with themselves motivate the students to learn more.

In the beginning of a period of study, one should think about each student's individual objectives, and draft their tests according to them, if necessary. For example, if Amy's goal in mathematics has been only learning certain parts of the content, her test should only measure her knowledge of this. Many students also get nervous about tests and find them anxiety-inducing. The situation should be gone through with them before the test itself to alleviate the nervousness. For students like Amy, anxiety can be increased if the test covers a lot of content, the content is too difficult, or they do not have the necessary strategies to prepare for the test.

The low-achievers' preparation for tests can be differentiated, for example by narrowing the content down individually. It is important to remember that if the teacher has drafted a specialised test for a student like Amy, it is unnecessary for her to revise the whole content for the test that is given to the rest of the class. The student can, for example, be given the topics that will be in their test, so that the student's revision will be concentrated on the correct content. They can even be given the test paper to take home so they can revise exactly what is needed. For low-achievers, the test can contain only a few things they have learned, such as a couple chapters' worth of mathematics or foreign language content. This can make studying clearer for the student, and they can revise and practice things for the test more easily.

It is important to pay attention to different strategies to study and prepare for a test. We have written briefly about these things in Chapters 5 and 8. One should go through different means of practising for a test with the whole class. One can go through these with low-achievers individually and in more depth. One should also give them written instructions for preparation. They can be glued on the inside of the cover of the book. This way, they can also be used by the parents as they support their child's preparation for a test.

IMAGE 5. A test situation without a differentiating attitude does not give every student equal opportunity to show what they can do

The test situation itself should be differentiated. The student should be given enough time to complete the test. If it is hard for the student to complete the test in a large group, they can complete it during breaks or in remedial education after school. Sometimes, one can give the test for the student to complete at home.

In a test situation, one should make sure that everyone has understood the questions in the test. The teacher can complete the test with the student, so that the student can verbalise their thought process out loud. One can also use a learning assistant in this, and the student can complete the test in a different space, which makes it easier for them to verbalise their answers. One should also not slam the whole test paper in front of a low-achiever, but give them one question at a time. It might be justified to complete the test in small parts during the day with some students.

Especially with young students, one should approach a test as a learning situation. According to their objectives, low-achievers can be let to complete the test in a small group, so that they can support each other's learning. One can also ask a low-achiever to complete as much of the test as possible by themselves, and then to use the book as support for the rest. This way, the test is also a learning activity. From the perspective of assessment, the teacher can mark the questions the student answered alone with a coloured pencil before the student completes the rest with the book.

When grading tests, one should remember the objectives of the test questions. For example, humanities subjects, such as history, where one needs to answer with a short essay, can be very hard for linguistically weak students. In this case, students can be let to answer using bullet points or numbered lists. Overall, one should not focus on the quality of writing in a test, or deduct points for grammar mistakes. In addition, it is good to think whether it is always necessary to give a score or grade for the test. Would it be beneficial to sometimes only give written feedback on a test? This can reduce the amount of work needed for the teacher to check the tests. Instead of counting a certain number of correct points in a history essay question, the teacher can look at the answer as a whole and give general feedback for the whole answer. We have personally used stamps to assess the content of an answer. A model answer to a question gets four stamps, whereas a more limited answer only gets two.

One should also pay attention to how one gives the tests back. For some students, the test can be handed back as it is. However, with many students, it is good to go through it verbally. This has a directive effect on learning. Sometimes, one can also go through the test with the whole class.

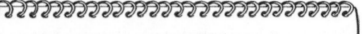

Differentiating the test situation – 101

- Differentiate preparation for a test by limiting the content covered or giving the student the test questions or instructions for how to revise for the test.
- Only test when necessary.
- Draft individualised tests with specific learning goals if needed.
- Let students come up with test questions by themselves.
- Give extra time for completing the test.
- Have the test during breaks, remedial education, or as a take-home test.
- Give the opportunity to answer questions verbally.
- Let low-achievers complete the test in pairs or small groups.
- Return the test individually, if necessary.

PORTFOLIO ASSESSMENT. Portfolio assessment is another form of assessment, in which the students have portfolios of their work, in which they accumulate more completed work throughout the year. One can compile test papers, essays, self-assessments and other work in the portfolio. For example, students can gather five things per subject that best reflect their knowledge and document them as they wish. For example, for science, the student can include a test that went very well, a video recording of their presentation, their notebook or workbook, a group project and a self-assessment in their portfolio.

A portfolio can be electronic, and it works in documenting the student's assessments. The portfolio is especially good in differentiating, as everyone can compile it individually based on their own strengths. In addition, one can easily return to look at the different steps of the learning process, and one can use it to show the student the progress they are making, for example at the end of the semester. Especially if a student has a negative perspective of themselves as a learner, portfolio assessment is a very good way to show the student how they have progressed and succeeded. With a portfolio, this is clearer than with a traditional test. Even the parents have an easier time tracking the student's progress using a portfolio.

PEDAGOGICAL DISCUSSIONS. One can also practice assessments verbally. Sometimes, a teacher can sit down with the student and parents, as well as other staff like school counsellors or student welfare officials. These situations are called assessment discussions and they are meetings in which the student's learning can be directed. Different kind of meetings should be held as often as needed. For example, a student like Amy may require a meeting in the beginning of a term, where goals and the means to achieve them are set together with the student and parents. At the end of the term, a new meeting can be held to assess the learning. In this case, one meeting would not be enough. The goals cannot be assessed if they have not been clearly set and understood by the student.

When done smartly, assessment discussions can give the teacher an opportunity to focus on the strengths of the student and bring up areas for improvement constructively, while taking the feelings of the student and parents into account. In addition, this direct communication between the teacher and the home gives the student and parents an opportunity to ask questions and give their perspective on school work and learning. Thus, the assessment discussion makes families and students committed to learning and study. For example, Ramus would benefit from regular discussions, in which his education is assessed with the parents. This makes it easier to coordinate models of behaviour at school and at home. If the collaboration between the school and the home is difficult, the teacher does not have to be the only representative of the school in the discussion, but one can ask the principal, another teacher, or a learning assistant to join in. This way, things said and agreed on in the discussion are known to others than only the teacher and parents.

LEARNING JOURNAL. A learning journal is a good way to differentiate assessment both for low and high-achievers. The teacher and student alike can use a learning journal to track learning and the development of thinking. With a learning journal, the teacher can also direct their teaching more towards both low and high-achievers. The learning journal can also be differentiated. For example, a high-achiever like Catherine can keep their journal up-to-date consistently. In the journal, they can reflect on their learning and thought in great depth. Another option for high-achievers is writing the journal in a foreign language. Low-achievers like Amy can keep a video journal, in which they reflect on their learning verbally. Some students can write in their journal every day, while others do this only once a week. Similarly, some students can reflect on their overall learning, while others reflect on a specific subject or theme.

PRESENTATIONS AND PROJECTS. Assessment should be practiced in relation to learning objectives. Often, different projects or presentations direct the students naturally towards the thing that is being learned according to their goals. Thus, presentations and projects are a very good means for assessment. For example, in history, one of the objectives is to learn historical periods and concepts related to them. If a student does a presentation on Ancient Greece, the topic does not always have to be assessed with a summative test afterwards. A benefit of projects or presentations is that a student can create them based on their interests and capabilities. In addition, a student who gets test anxiety and underachieves, can be summatively assessed only based on the presentation, even though other students take a test on that content.

HOMEWORK. It is good to remember that even homework and their observations are a good method for assessment. However, in the hustle and bustle of everyday life, a teacher does not always have time to check the students' homework very carefully. It is possible to differentiate this method as well, and one does not have to use the same approach with all students. For example, the teacher can only collect certain students' work at regular intervals to check them carefully. The teacher can easily assess Amy's homework to see what she still needs to practice, and take this into consideration in teaching. Differentiation of projects and homework is explored in-depth in Chapter 4.

COMMON GOALS REACHED INDIVIDUALLY. Differentiated assessment does not always have to mean that different things are being assessed. The class can set common targets in a very heterogeneous group. Then, a student can collect points or check marks for themselves or for a group. For example, one can reach the highest grade in mathematics by completing 100 problems during a period of study. Then, an individually progressing student's problems should naturally be fit to their goals. The problems themselves can be different or students can be required to complete a different number of problems in order to reach the grade. A common goal could also be taking others into consideration. Catherine can collect points by helping others, while Sam and Rasmus can get recognition even for not actively bothering others.

Ideas for differentiated assessment

- Testing with differentiated arrangements
- Self and peer assessment
- Portfolio
- Assessment discussions and meetings
- A learning journal, either written or in vlog form
- Presentations and projects
- Homework as means for assessment
- Clearly illustrated, verbalised and commonly set goals
- The individual fulfilment of goals, either by quality or quantity

In this chapter, we brought up some practical assessment methods and explored the ways they can be differentiated. As we said in the beginning of the chapter, there are many different ways of assessment, and the only important thing while choosing between one method and another is whether those methods can give you the necessary information about the student's knowledge and skills. We encourage you to use a wide variety of assessments in teaching. In addition, one should remember that one does not have to assess every student in the same way. For some students, a test is a very good means for assessment in a certain situation, whereas others can benefit more from keeping a learning journal.

Tips to remedy the starting point

GRADE 1 & 3: SAM AND RASMUS

- Set goals together with the student.
- Make sure that the student has understood the objectives.
- Use as large a variety in assessments as possible.
- Give positive feedback and make successes visible immediately.
- Practice self and peer assessment with students.
- Hold assessment discussions with parents and the student.

GRADE 5: AMY

- Have tests only occasionally. Differentiate the test situation and the preparation for it.
- Offer an opportunity for verbal assessment.
- Offer different opportunities to demonstrate skills, such as projects and presentations.
- Periodically, check through homework carefully. This will direct you in later teaching.
- Focus on strengths and emphasise positive feedback.

GRADE 9: CATHERINE

- Make sure that goals have been set properly.
- Make sure that assessment measures the set goals.
- Set goals higher with the student.
- Direct to keep a learning journal.
- Direct to keep an up-to-date portfolio.

Part 4

DIFFERENTIATION IN DIFFERENT SUBJECTS

In Part IV of this book, we will look into differentiating different subjects in detail. Because the book progresses cumulatively in terms of differentiation, it is assumed that the reader has become familiar with Part III of the book, in which there are practical tips for different areas of differentiation in subjects mentioned in this part. In Part IV, we have chosen to discuss subjects that are needed in learning other subjects. Language and literature is necessary for all subjects, and mathematics creates a basis for other STEM subjects. In foreign languages, new content is based on content that has been learned previously, and the importance of knowing languages is highlighted in further education. Moreover, based on our experience, differentiating language and literature, mathematics and foreign languages is often most challenging for teachers.

Each chapter focuses on one subject. Chapter 8 addresses language and literature. Chapter 9 covers differentiation in mathematics. In turn, Chapter 10 is focused on differentiating foreign languages. It should be noted that differentiation of these subjects should be approached through the 5D model while not forgetting the general principles of differentiation, such as differentiating the learning environment or instructions.

8. LANGUAGE AND LITERATURE

The starting point

GRADE 1: SAM

Sam has a hard time following teaching in language and literature class. His restlessness makes it hard to learn how to read and write, because he cannot always focus on practicing reading or writing by hand. He was excited about school at first, but the excitement has turned into anxiety, which has begun to show negatively in Sam's mood at school.

GRADE 3: RASMUS

Rasmus is linguistically talented, and he does not have challenges with grammar. However, Rasmus does not like language and literature classes, because he dislikes writing. Rasmus is a good reader, but he would rather read comic books, and gets frustrated with reading chapter books. Social situations are difficult for Rasmus, and he has challenges in taking others into consideration.

GRADE 5: AMY

Language and literature is a hard subject for Amy. Processing certain sounds is hard for her, which shows at word level. Amy has difficulties in spelling words correctly. Amy's reading is slow and flawed compared to her age group average. Amy is also shy to express herself, and does not trust her linguistic skills.

GRADE 9: CATHERINE

Catherine finds language and literature lessons easy. She is an excellent reader and writer. She also has good communication skills. She can listen to others and justify her opinions. Catherine completes work in class very quickly, and she feels like language and literature teaching does not challenge her enough.

In the first chapter of Part IV, we will focus on differentiation in language and literature. We have divided the chapter into three themes: reading, writing and communication. In the end, we will take a short look at other things one should consider when differentiating language and literature teaching. In this chapter, we will explore differentiation of language and literature teaching rather generally. Supportive equipment for reading and writing, such as coloured sheets and electronic devices, have been introduced in Chapter 6. In addition, the teaching arrangements explored in Chapter 5 are an integral part of differentiating language and literature teaching.

IMAGE 6. The general principles of differentiated instruction are highlighted in teaching language and literature

READING

The reading and writing skills of students vary, and they develop at different rates. Thus, each student should have the opportunity to progress individually at school. Especially with young students, it is unnecessary to rush teaching language and literature skills. However, it is good to give periodic remedial education to low-achievers in order to develop the students' linguistic skills.

Reading develops and is refined best by reading, so it is incredibly important to motivate even the low-achievers to read. Having a wide variety of stimulating reading material available in the classroom serves the differentiation of reading. In a classroom of small students, it is good to have little books for different levels of readers. In primary education, magnetic or wooden letters can motivate weak readers. It is important to arouse an interest in language and literature for the future. Even for older students, it would be good to have a lot of literature at different levels, from comic books to non-fiction.

In reading, one should remember that, according to the principles of differentiated instruction, not all students have to always read the same text. Weak readers, or students who dislike reading, can be motivated by using different texts, as all kinds of reading develops one's abilities to read. Younger children in particular are often more motivated by comic books than novels. There is less text in them, and they can thus be used to motivate weak and demotivated readers. In comics, the story is also told through pictures, which helps to support the written text. However, it is good to encourage students to read different kinds of texts. As the reading develops, the pictures of a comic book can make a student lazy, if one wants them to understand text specifically.

Low-achievers can be given the same text to read as homework for multiple days. As students read a familiar text, they begin to recognise more and more words each time, which makes reading more fluent. This can have a positive impact on the student's perception of themselves as a learner. It is good to direct students like Catherine towards a wide variety of literature. While exploring different genres of literature, such as poetry or non-fiction, students like Catherine can focus on more difficult written works. As extra practice for high-achievers, one can ask them to keep a blog for book reviews when they finish a book.

Sometimes, students can bring a text from home that they enjoy reading. Alternatively, the teacher can choose texts to read based on the students' areas of interest. For example, a student like Rasmus, who is clever but unmotivated, would be happier to work with a text about his favourite band, compared to the regular textbook text. When motivating students, one can try different kinds of incentives and prizes. Sometimes, one can agree with the student that once they have read a certain book, the class can watch it as a movie.

Different reading diplomas work well in differentiating reading, as students can commonly choose the books they read by themselves. Small students naturally need help and direction at first. Alternatively, the teacher can draft differentiated reading lists for low and high-achievers. For example, one can allow low-achievers a certain number of audiobooks or books read by the parents. One can differentiate a reading diploma by giving common themes for the books. For example, during the first week, one has to read a book about some kind of an animal. During the second week, the students have to read their favourite book or story. This way, students can choose books based on their reading level from similar topics. The important thing is to wake up the students' excitement about reading, even for low-achievers. Thus, a reading diploma can be differentiated based on the number and difficulty of books.

Different teaching arrangement, such as flexible grouping, can be used when differentiating reading (see Chapter 3). During class, students can be sometimes grouped according to their level of reading. While weaker readers read a plain language text with the teacher in the back of the classroom, other students can read their own books with noise-cancelling headphones or earmuffs on. Students can read a book out loud, one at a time, and the teacher can also read some of it while the students listen and keep track of where the teacher is going in the text. Reading a book together makes discussing the content of the book and explaining difficult words possible.

It works best if everyone reads the same book; high-achievers can read the original version, while low-achievers can read the plain text version. This makes it possible to discuss the book with the whole class. Book discussions can be done in many ways, such as in the form of a play. Simplified texts and stories can be fairly easy to find online. A good method is to form pairs containing one weak and one strong reader. The weak reader can read some of the text out loud, whereas the strong reader can read a bigger passage, while the weaker reader follows the text while listening. Older students can be directed to read with those at a lower grade level, or they can practice dramatic reading by going to read stories to pre-schoolers or those in first or second grade.

Computers or tablets, which were mentioned in Chapter 6, can also be used to differentiate reading. Some students have an easier time reading off a screen, because they can enlarge the font size. In addition, many students like Rasmus might feel more motivated when they get to use electronic devices to read, instead of a traditional book. Often, beginner readers with dyslexia can find it difficult to connect phonemes to one another. The teacher can highlight certain phonemes with different colours, or make them bigger on the screen. For example, students like Amy can benefit from highlighting certain spelling patterns, which also supports getting them right while writing.

In addition to language and literature, reading is highlighted in all subject in which reading and writing are needed. This includes almost all subjects, apart from the arts or physical education. Because of this, traditional education is heavily reading and writing based, and a child with dyslexia is very unequal in comparison with their peers. Teaching reading strategies fits well in language and literature class, but it should also be done during other lessons. Surprisingly often, reading strategies have not automatised even with students in higher grade levels.

Reading strategies mean different techniques a student can use to make sense of and understand the text they read. Different strategies should be practiced as a group, but they are especially highlighted with those students who have difficulties in absorbing long texts that are read in language and literature or the humanities. Individual reading strategies can also be developed with low-achievers, for example in remedial education. One can write these strategies down for the low-achiever, so that they can glue it in their notebook or stick it on their desk. Often, students start to read a new chapter from the beginning, without scanning the text first. It would be good to teach students to read the title first and to think what the chapter might remind them of. Potential pictures, graphs or sub-titles can also give clues as to what the text is about, which makes comprehending the text easier. In addition, in textbooks, there are often summary boxes at the end of a chapter that summarise the key parts of the text. Often, low-achievers need guidance and practice at first, so that they can use the summary boxes in their studying, or, for example, while revising for a test.

For low-achievers, useful reading strategies include finding and underlining the most important sentence in a paragraph and circling all difficult or new words so that they can be explained later, either in pairs or together as a class. Students can also ask their partner questions about the text. One can teach older students to write a short summary about the key points after they have read the text. High-achievers can do this in full sentences, while low-achievers can write short bullet points. Alternatively, one can create a mind map to summarise the key points of the chapter. Reading strategies can be used with non-fiction texts, such as history or science, or with fictional texts in literature.

The support of the home is highlighted especially while differentiating language and literature for low-achievers. Parents should be encouraged to read to their children as much as possible, in order to awaken an interest towards reading and language. If a student can already read a little, one can recommend the parent to read together with the child, so that the child can read a couple of sentences from the book according to their reading level, while the parent then reads the rest of the chapter to them.

Tips to differentiate reading

- Offer students a stimulating reading environment.
- Utilise the students' own texts.
- Have a reading lesson weekly and choose the students' books individually.
- Group students flexibly into different reader groups.
- Sometimes, pair low and high-achievers together and utilise peer support.
- Motivate to read through different games or incentives.
- Read the book together with low-achievers. Read bits out loud yourself sometimes.
- Guide students to read different kinds of texts and to analyse what they have read.
- Utilise plain language texts.
- Utilise information technology while reading.
- Teach students different reading strategies. Write the strategies down, step-by-step, for low-achievers.
- Involve parents in supporting reading.

WRITING

In differentiated instruction, everyone should get a chance to study according to their skills. This includes writing. When differentiating writing in language and literature class, the easiest way for the teacher is to use the same activity but to differentiate its execution. An example of this is dictation, in which the teacher reads out a word, and students write it down. The weakest of young students can only write the beginning or end syllables of each word, whereas others write down the whole word. Dictations can also be differentiated so that high-achievers are asked to use the dictated words in a sentence. For older students, low-achievers can write down the first few words of each sentence, whereas high-achievers can be directed to come up with a subordinate clause for each dictated sentence. Doing this means that the teacher does not have to hold three different dictations. The same principle can be applied to other activities in language and literature lessons.

In writing, it is important to acknowledge the students' possible emotional reactions and how they affect learning. For example, detailed correction of all mistakes and highlighting each missing letter are often not purposeful while correcting a story writing assignment by a student who finds writing challenging. This can lead to negativity in the student's attitude or lack of motivation towards writing. If one wants to focus on grammar rules and correct spelling, one can conduct appropriate activities for this, for example in remedial education. Of course, one does not have to be completely absolute about the situation, and one should consider the students' individual temperaments. Some students want every mistake in their text to be corrected. In addition, if there is no punctuation in the text at all, the student should be reminded of this. As we have written before, one can progress in spelling step by step, or focus on one aspect at once.

Overall, it is important to give even the low-achievers a feeling that they can be an active part of language and literature lessons and develop their creative expression. For example, students can dictate stories, while the teacher, learning assistant or a peer acts as a scribe. Together, a low and a high-achiever can verbally compose a story, while the high-achiever is in charge of writing it down. One can also give a short beginning of a story for a low-achiever, for which they need to come up with an ending. A student in need of strong differentiation can be given a story, in which there are gaps for single words, which the student can fill in to create a complete story. This kind of differentiation works especially for a newly arrived immigrant student who is only beginning to learn the language. For example, one can give the student lyrics to a song in the language of instruction, from which all the verbs are missing. The student can listen to the song and fill in the gaps based on their hearing comprehension and explain what the words mean to the teacher.

Sometimes, free story-writing can cause blocks, especially in older students. Drama is a good way to open these blocks. If writing feels difficult, one can tell and act out stories before writing them down. When the storyline is clear, as the story has been come up with as a group, each student can write the story down according to their own skills. Before writing the story down, the story can be revised and, if necessary, its key points can be written down on the board for everyone to see. Low-achievers can write one sentence per event in the story, while high-achievers can be encouraged to go into detail and to even come up with more events to fit into the story.

Keeping a diary is a differentiated writing practice. For example, every Monday, young students can write in their diaries about the most important events of their weekend in a few sentences. This can be differentiated based on the students' skills. The highest achievers can produce long passages regarding their weekend, using complex grammatical structures. However, lowest achievers can only be expected to produce a few short sentences. This activity can even be used with first graders. Then, the student can write down single words to describe their weekend. The teacher can write down words that those students can copy who cannot write yet. Students can also illustrate the events of their weekend as drawings. For example, one could agree on a certain number of sentences with a student like Rasmus, and after that let him draw the rest.

Overall, different projects are good for differentiating language and literature teaching, as students can choose their topics based on their interests, and create products that match their skills. For example, while writing about favourite hobbies with young students, low-achievers can be directed to produce only single words, whereas high-achievers can be asked to produce logically progressing text. Often, it is natural to use collaborative work methods in project work. Then, every student can take part in the activity in a differentiated way. An example of this kind of a project is publishing a class newspaper, which is easy to differentiate both for low and high-achievers. For example, a student who is good at drawing but slow to read and write can be in charge of illustrating the newspaper or drawing a comic. High-achievers like Catherine can be in charge of designing the newspaper, writing the articles and managing its production as editor-in-chief. One can use flexible grouping in a newspaper project, and it can be extended to multiple classes, or even the whole school. This way, there can be students from different grade levels in the same group. Especially with young students, it works best if one gives them certain roles in the work. One can be an illustrator, another a researcher, a third student can be a writer, and the fourth can present the product to the editor-in-chief. Roles make work clearer and make students more committed to the work. One should listen to the students' wishes and visions when planning this kind of a project.

One can utilise information technology when differentiating writing. While writing on a word processing programme, a low-achiever can easily spot their mistakes, and one can edit and add to the text later on more easily. In class, while others are working by hand, low-achievers can, on occasion, write a story by computer. If the objective of the lesson is to learn a grammatical structure or write a story, one can occasionally let low-achievers use a computer. If the lesson objectives are related to fine motor skills, writing by hand is appropriate. It is important to keep the individual goals of each student in mind in all teaching. For some students, it is a success when they can produce text one can understand in the first place. From other students, one can expect tidy handwriting.

Tips to differentiate writing

- Differentiate in common dictation exercises based on the students' skills.
- Encourage students to express themselves in writing. Do not curb their enthusiasm by being overly critical of mistakes.
- Let the student dictate stories, while a learning assistant or a peer, for example, acts as a scribe.
- Direct a low-achiever to write a story together with a high-achiever.
- Offer the student a pre-written beginning for a story for them to complete.
- Use drama to orientate students to write.
- Have students write in a diary based on individual goals.
- Execute open writing assignments.
- Use collaborative projects, in which everyone can take part based on their skills. An example of this can be a newspaper published by the class, or even the whole school.
- Use a computer to differentiate writing.

COMMUNICATION

Listening to others and expressing one's own opinions in a constructive way are important skills needed while communicating with other people. However, many students like Rasmus need a lot of practice in these skills. In addition, challenges with naming can cause problems in communication. It would be important to practice different situations at school, in which one needs to communicate clearly. Many methods in this chapter can be used in teaching languages, but also to differentiate communicative situations in any subject.

Society and the school system traditionally favour students who are outgoing and linguistically talented. However, even introverted and shy people can have communication skills that are not easily seen. We will explore communication mostly from the perspective of introverted students, since without differentiation of communicative situations, these kinds of students often underachieve at school.

At school, the role of a teacher is vital in a situation where communication is needed. Often, especially students with dyslexia have challenges even with the comprehension of spoken word. Then, the teacher's clear communication is highlighted in teaching. In Chapter 5, we emphasised the clarity of giving instructions. One should pay attention to one's speech, especially to speed, coherency and supporting speech with expressions and gestures. One should also remember the context of the speech. For example, when giving important instructions, one should be clear and concise with one's speech, whereas in dramatic story-telling, one can use more vivid language.

It is important in terms of the students' affective, or emotional factors, that no one is forced or pressured into an anxiety-inducing situation in which one has to speak. Some students can, for one reason or another, exhibit selective mutism at school, which can be very challenging for teachers. However, this is rather rare, as selectively mute students are approximately one in 200 (Lämsä & Erkolahti 2013). It is also important to remember, that quiet or selectively mute students should not be made feel bad for not talking. One should talk about this actively in the school community, with the permission of the parents. It is also important to let all teachers who teach a selectively mute student know about special practices, in order to avoid difficult situations. We have used a laminated note that a selectively mute student could show to an unfamiliar adult at school, especially when the teacher suddenly changes or when the student is interacting with an unfamiliar teacher in the hallway.

When dealing with introverted and quiet students, it is good to think about seating arrangements. A working solution could be to seat a student like that next to a good friend, so that the student can write answers down and their friend can read them out. Sometimes, the student can be ready to whisper the answer to the friend, who can then let the whole class know. Alternatively, one can agree on differentiated answering practices with the students. For example, we have had students, with whom we have agreed on a few different signals when the student wants to answer, depending on whether the student wants to answer out loud or not. The student can, for example, put their left hand up when they know the answer but do not want to say it out loud, and put their right hand up when they feel safe enough to talk. Students should be encouraged after even a small verbal communication, and not be corrected for any possible grammatical mistakes.

Most students are likely to feel nervous about performing in front of an audience, but for a shy student like Amy, who has dyslexia, they can be especially anxiety-inducing. Presentation and performance situations can be differentiated, for example, by letting students give their presentation in a group, and the quiet student's spoken part can be considerably shorter than others. The student can have a helper, who can read the texts while the student shows pictures. Sometimes even the teacher can read the presentation, either as a whole or parts of it, while the student presents visual materials to support the presentation. Some students are only mute at school, but talk normally at home or during their free time. Then, a student can record or take a video of the presentation beforehand and show it to others at school. The student can also be given an opportunity to only present to a few friends or only the teacher.

With differentiation, the students should be in an environment in which they can work naturally, even when not speaking. Speaking and presentation situations are still important to practice in a safe environment, in order to avoid making those situations even more dreadful for the student. In addition, it is important to remember that even communication skills can be developed in remedial education. For example, students who dread performing can practice different communication and presentation scenarios in a small group, in a safe environment. In addition, students like Amy can play games, such as Charades or Taboo, because they develop verbal skills and naming, and are often popular among students.

When there is an air of trust in the classroom, speaking can become easier, too. However, it is important to distinguish between students who really are genuinely selectively mute and those students who use talking as a means of power or authority. We have experience with students who have decided to not speak for days after a conflict, because they were afraid of negative consequences. Just like in all differentiation, knowing one's students and collaboration with the home are highlighted here. Often, appropriate flexibility works better than being absolute. We do not mean that one should stray too far from common ground rules, but rather offering a student an apparent choice. This also works for lower secondary school students. It is useless to insist on a student talking, unless it is completely necessary. The selective mutism can be left without attention, and the teacher can periodically offer an opportunity to take part in conversations without making it into a big deal.

Taking part in a communication scenario usually feels safer in a small group than a large one. One should include a lot of pair or group work in teaching, in order to allow shy and quiet students to participate better. One can systematically use one language and literature lesson per week to practice communication skills. A working practice that makes differentiation easier are discussions in the style of a Socratic seminar, in which students can learn to listen, wait for their own turn and state their own opinion. With small students, topics can be simple, such as telling others about their weekend.

However, older students can talk about more difficult topics as well. This can be practiced within the class, or even with other classes from the same grade level. For example, one can use a parallel lesson arrangement for an exercise like this, in order to have the seminar amongst multiple classes. This exercise can be differentiated with flexible grouping. Students can be divided into small groups in different areas of the classroom, so that each student can engage in the conversation more. Occasionally, it is good to group high-achievers together, so they can engage in high level of conversation, for example in the form of a debate. Then, the teacher can focus more on supporting low-achiever groups. In addition, for students like Rasmus, who have difficulties in social situations, it is good to start communication lessons with a small group of three, or only with one partner. Students should also be grouped based on interests, so the groups can choose their own topics of discussion. This practice increases a positive atmosphere at school, when students get to know each other better. Flexible grouping and parallel lessons have been explored in Chapter 3.

In order to differentiate communication skills for high-achievers, one can have students do projects, in which they also use other linguistic skills. For a student like Catherine, one can assign a project in which students practice being a reporter. Students can come up with a topic of their choice, and make an article or a news clip, by interviewing people at school and in their free time. Students can write the interview questions by themselves, and record or take a video of the interview, for example by using a tablet. This kind of project also supports transdisciplinary learning.

There are many methods to practice skills in communication and emotional intelligence. One can also consult a school counsellor or psychologist about these. In our own school, the counsellor and psychologist have sometimes gotten involved with leading these lessons for whole classes or specific students. The results from this kind of a collaboration have been excellent. One should also think about different ways to support the students' verbal expression together with them.

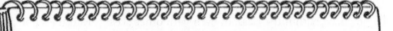

Tips to differentiate communication

- Pay attention to the clarity of your own communication.
- Use one lesson per week to practice communication skills. Group students flexibly.
- Pay attention to the seating arrangements.
- Execute discussions in pairs and small groups. Change the groups periodically.
- If needed, give remedial education regarding communication skills and scenarios.
- Motivate and encourage even the smallest amount of speech.
- Use different linguistic games to practice communication.
- Build a learning environment, in which shy and selectively mute students are supported.
- Give an opportunity to answer in different ways, such as in writing or through pictures.
- Differentiate presentations so that a student can present with a partner, alone to the teacher, or through a pre-made video.
- Offer high-achievers different projects, for example presentations and interviews.
- Consult and utilise the school counsellor and psychologist.

OTHER NOTABLE ISSUES

Differentiating homework was explored in Chapter 5. However, in this case, we would like to highlight a few things about homework, specifically in language and literature. Even in language and literature, homework should be approached based on the students' skills and goals. Especially in lower grade levels, students are often given homework that involves reading. However, some students can take much longer to read the same text as others. Because of this, it might be easier to assign a specific time that each student should spend reading the text. One can also differentiate by assigning high-achievers reading homework from a fiction or non-fiction novel instead of a common text. If possible, one should also utilise the students' own interests.

Language and literature homework should be assigned individually. For example, a low-achiever's homework assignment could be to play a language and literature related game at home for ten minutes each day. Common homework can also be differentiated by allowing students to answer written work with only a few words or to complete them orally. When done orally, the homework can be checked by the parents, who can mark the homework as completed in the notebook. Appropriate practice is, of course, incredibly important for low-achievers. Thus, one can also compromise with the students and agree that every other language and literature homework can be completed orally, while the rest are completed in writing. This way the students can also practice writing without being overwhelmed. Simultaneously, the student gets the feeling that they can affect their own learning and that their individuality has been taken into account.

One should also differentiate the use of workbooks and textbooks in the language and literature. One can expect low-achievers to only complete a few questions, whereas the highest achievers can complete some extra questions in which skills are applied. A low-achiever can answer single questions with one or a few words, while high-achievers must give their answers in full sentences and justify their answers. A student who struggles with writing can also complete some tasks verbally. This topic was explored in more detail in Chapter 5.

Even in language and literature, one can use learning materials from different grade levels. As we already noted in Chapter 5, language and literature teaching often follows a spiral structure, in which certain themes repeat themselves in different breadth and depth in different grade levels. Thus, it might be justified for low-achievers to use materials from lower grade levels to support the material of their own grade level. Similarly, high-achievers can be given more challenging extra tasks from books from higher grade levels. One can also use plain language materials with those students with linguistic challenges.

In grammar tests, one should give low-achievers the opportunity to answer verbally. For example, the dyslexia of students like Amy should be taken into consideration in a test. One can, for example, read the questions out loud to her. The student can also complete the test in a separate space with a teacher or learning assistant, or during breaks in the classroom with their own teacher.

In conclusion, there are many methods to differentiate language and literature, which can offer more individualised teaching for both low and high-achievers. Teaching that is too difficult or easy can cause frustration and a negative attitude towards school. It is good to keep in mind that arousing students' interest in language and literature is a notable goal in itself. Differentiated teaching that corresponds to one's own level motivates students and directs them to get interested in language and literature.

Tips to remedy the starting point

GRADE 1: SAM

- Give remedial education, both pro-actively and reactively.
- Limit the number of tasks.
- Differentiate homework.
- Group students flexibly and offer individualised teaching.
- Keep Sam's language and literature teaching sessions short and vary activities.
- Let Sam dictate stories to the teacher, the learning assistant, or one of his peers.
- Get Sam excited about reading by using easy and short books, and by reading a lot out loud.

GRADE 3: RASMUS

- Limit the number of written activities.
- Let Rasmus write with a computer.
- Let Rasmus complete some written tasks verbally.
- Have a periodic reading lessons. Motivate Rasmus to read by using comic books.
- Keep the amount of homework light.

GRADE 5: AMY

- Use materials from lower grade levels or plain text materials.
- Differentiate the amount and level of tasks.
- Give remedial education, both pro-actively and reactively.
- Give individualised homework.
- Let Amy record an answer to a written question. Increase opportunities for different kinds of answers, even in test.
- Do not pay too much attention to grammar and spelling mistakes in creative writing.
- Direct to write a story with a partner.
- Offer pre-written beginnings to a story.
- Utilise plain language books.
- Teach individualised reading strategies.

GRADE 9: CATHERINE

- Offer work from higher grade level books.
- Direct to read more challenging books and to write reviews for the books she reads.
- Direct to write a blog or a learning journal.
- Encourage to create wide-ranging projects and presentations.

9. MATHEMATICS

The starting point

GRADE 1: SAM

Mathematics is one of Sam's least favourite subjects, because he has to sit still during those lessons. Sam can usually focus on only a few problems, after which he starts to bother others by talking and walking around. He has trouble with focusing on teacher-led instruction as well, and things written on the board are usually lost on him. Sam also cannot wait for his turn or be quiet during the teacher's instruction.

GRADE 3: RASMUS

Rasmus becomes anxious in mathematics class when presented with two pages of work in the workbook. He does not want to solve the problems, and begins to argue with the teacher over the number of problems he needs to complete. These situations often cause a block, in which Rasmus gets upset and becomes aggressive which consequently hinders him to complete his tasks during the lessons.

GRADE 5: AMY

Mathematics is a difficult subject for Amy. Even the basic problems are left undone, with verbal and applied maths problems being especially difficult for her. Often, Amy does not have enough time to complete any verbal problems during class, and has to complete them at home. Basic calculations have not been automatised, so she makes a lot of mistakes in long additions and subtractions. In addition, it is hard for Amy to remember her times tables, so she often mechanically calculates them using addition.

GRADE 9: CATHERINE

Mathematics is easy for Catherine. During lessons, everyone works on the same page at the same time. Catherine can always complete the basic and extra problems of the workbook during the lesson. The teacher never gives her more challenging work. Sometimes Catherine uses the rest of the class to draw in her notebook or help her peers. She gets bored in class very easily. Catherine has begun to take understanding the problems for granted, and cannot always be bothered to complete all problems.

Mathematics is one of the integral subjects in most school systems. For one reason or another, out of many subjects it is often mathematics that makes people react strongly. For some, it is their absolute favourite subject, whereas others hate it so much it gives them anxiety. The negative emotional reaction regarding mathematics is called mathematical anxiety (Mononen, Aunio, Väisänen, Korhonen & Tapola 2017). It is clear that negative emotional reactions have a negative effect on learning. However, one can prevent mathematical anxiety by differentiated practices. We believe that by differentiating mathematics teaching, one can reduce the number of people who will later remember always hating mathematics at school.

Mathematical learning difficulties, or challenges in learning basic calculations, cause an obstacle for education. The difficulties in mathematics can manifest alone or be combined with weak linguistic abilities. It is difficult to estimate the number of mathematical learning difficulties in students due to different definitions, but based on some estimates, specific learning difficulties, or dyscalculia, can be found in 5-7%, and milder challenges in 10-15% of students (Aunio 2014; Räsänen 2012). Mathematical anxiety has been estimated to affect almost 1 in 6 students (Ashcraft, Krause & Hopko 2007).

In Part III of this book, we have already occasionally referred to differentiating mathematics, for example in the context of completing tasks and homework. However, in this chapter, we will address the topic in more detail. At first, we will focus on the general issues one should consider in mathematics, as well as the overall support of mathematics at school. After this, we will present practical support tools for mathematics teaching, and explore the differentiation of mathematics homework and testing.

GENERAL ISSUES IN TEACHING MATHEMATICS

As we noted in Chapter 5, one should create a differentiated culture in the classroom, in which study is individualised and everyone does not have to progress at the same rate. Typically, workbooks define a great part of the content of mathematics lessons. The speed of teaching is usually fast, and often the whole class completes one chapter per lesson, which is challenging for many low-achievers. In differentiated mathematics teaching, it is possible to have the whole class work on a common book during some lessons, and some lessons are spent on individualised problems. However, in practice, the teacher can find constantly making individualised work burdening.

One can also differentiate in a smaller scale. Low-achievers can use the same book as the others most of the time, but sometimes they could practice basic operations alongside the workbook. The student could have a book from the lower grade level, which they can fill in to differentiate their learning. For example, students like Amy could complete the introductions to certain topics, and then consolidate that knowledge with individualised material, while other students get to know that topic at a deeper level.

Learning mathematics is based on skills that have been learned before. Thus, if the basics are challenging, it is not smart to progress onto harder topics with the student. Most workbooks support this practice, by having the first chapters of each theme to explore the basics, while becoming more challenging in the later chapters. This practice does not have to apply to everyone, but only those who need it the most. For instance, in Finland, the curriculum even urges teachers to give each student the opportunity for instruction also in the most central content areas of previous grades if they lack the sufficient command of them (FNCCBE 2014, section 14.4.4).

In mathematics teaching, it would be good to have a principle in which students can familiarise themselves with a common theme according to their capabilities. A good example of this is multiplication tables, which are troublesome for many students, as they require a lot of learning by heart. For example, 2nd and 3rd graders should first focus only on the easiest times tables, such as the multiples of 1, 2, 5, 9, and 10. This makes it easier for the students to automatise the operations. Once they have mastered these, the students will already know half of the times tables. In most education systems, times tables are a recurring theme every year, so low-achievers can learn the more challenging times tables in higher grade levels. Similarly, operations involving time are challenging for many students, because time is divided into 60 units, instead of the usual 10. It would be good to think whether low-achievers should first get to know a 12-hour clock, consolidate those skills, and then move onto a 24-hour clock, which is more challenging.

One can differentiate mathematics teaching, for example, through different teaching methods. Contractual project work, which we have mentioned in the earlier chapters, supports differentiation in mathematics very well. Then, each student can progress in their workbook as fast as they are able to, for a certain period of time. The teacher can teach new topics to small groups or individually. The student can take part in setting their own goals, and one does not necessarily have to have a test at all. For example, in our school, there has been a practice in grade 9 (students' age 15-16) geometry, in which 100 acceptably completed problems means the student will get the highest grade. Similarly, 50 problems means an accepted performance with that theme. Students have found this practice to be very motivating, and often there has been a more pleasant working atmosphere in the classroom during these lessons than in an average lesson.

Students like Sam or Rasmus, whose challenges lie in work habits instead of learning, should be differentiated individually with the work they complete. One should note that then, differentiation should focus on the number of problems, and not the level or content of the problems. A functional practice would be the kind, in which one agrees on a certain number of problems with the student in the beginning of the lesson, which the student must complete during the lesson. One should include only a few mechanical basic calculations in the student's list of mathematical problems, and include more applications and problem-solving questions. This way, one can avoid Rasmus and Sam only completing the basic problems and not working within their zone of proximal development at all.

High-achievers like Catherine should be also offered individual work, so they can work on material that is challenging enough. A high-achiever could have a workbook from a higher grade level that they could work on alongside the common workbook. They can work on that at the end of the lesson. There exists a lot of material that is not tied to a specific grade level, including problem-solving questions, which can be used with high-achievers.

In teacher-led instruction using the board, it is good to remember the differences in each student. For example, understanding the decimal system can be difficult for many students. It can be hard to understand what the number 478 is made of, and how many tens there are in it. Often, different workbook series mark ones, tens, hundreds and thousands in different colours, which makes understanding them a lot easier. The teacher should systematically use these same colours when working on the board. This makes the students understand which colour denotes which place value. The teacher should also include problems of different difficulties while working on the board, so that even low-achievers can follow teaching and take part in it. For example, when doing complex calculations, one should ask for answers to certain steps in the calculation, such as 4-2 or 5-3, from the low-achievers, so they also get a feeling of success. The decimal system should be explored in detail even in higher grades. Surprisingly, problems with mathematics often arise from the basics, such as the decimal system, not being understood properly.

There are teaching methods developed specifically for mathematics, in which a certain principle is followed. If following a specific teaching programme feels too difficult, one can still apply these principles to the differentiation of one's own teaching. For example, the Varga-Neményi method has many elements that serve low-achievers in mathematics. These methods can be tested alongside other teaching, for example in remedial education.

In addition, there are many different e-learning programmes and activities for mathematics. Some of them save the game, which helps the teacher with assessment, and some also edit the difficulty of the game based on the progress of the student, which automatically differentiates their learning. Games often motivate students, so they can also help with creating a positive outlook on mathematics. One can have a rule, where low-achievers can spend ten minutes of each mathematics lesson playing a certain maths game on the computer. In addition, the student's homework can include playing a certain game, either in addition or as an alternative to other mathematics homework.

Verbal problems cause a lot of grief for students like Amy. First of all, students can be confused about whether they should add, subtract, multiply or divide, in which case their answers can sound completely impossible. It is good to open up verbal problems together with low-achievers. Then, important words can be emphasised to support understanding. One should direct the student's own thinking by asking supporting questions, such as 'What does the problem ask you?', or 'What will you do first? What about after?'. The student should be directed to recognise key words from the problems, such as 'more' or 'altogether'. These can also be underlined with different colours. This way, by separating it into small parts, an application problem turns into a basic, mechanical problem for the student. For example, words 'how much more' or 'how much less' automatically mean subtraction.

One should teach the student to draw a picture or model of the problem. One should practice drawing these diagrams a lot, and this should also be allowed as an answer to a test. Often, the child can calculate the problem and understands what is asked, but cannot write down an expression for the problem. Consequently, it is always good to ask the student to explain verbally what they do while solving the problem. 'You added. Good. Why did you do so?' As they learn to verbalise their work, the students also learn to recognise the relationship between key words in the problem and the expression of the problem. For a student with dyslexia, one can make verbal problems easier and keep the language plain. One can sometimes give this for a student like Catherine to do. Students can also practice coming up with verbal problems for each other. These problems will most likely be appropriately difficult for everyone.

The best place for practising mathematics is the school, in which there is a professional teacher present. Thus, a low-achiever should move from basic problems to verbal problems with the support of the teacher, even if the basic problems were still incomplete. One can also use peer support in differentiating verbal problems, so that students can solve them in pairs or small groups. Sometimes one can use high-achievers by pairing them up with low-achievers. The students can solve similar problems, taking turns, while the other observes. In this situation, the low-achiever can get an example of the high-achiever's performance and the high-achiever can support the low-achiever's work, if needed. High-achievers must be taught not to give direct answers to the low-achiever. Instead, they should be taught to ask why one should, for example, add numbers together in a certain problem. Then, the teacher can focus on instructing those who need it the most.

Wider flexible grouping, in which students can be grouped across different grades into different groups based on what they need, is well-suited for differentiating mathematics. Flexible grouping can be practiced across grade levels, so that different-aged students can work together on challenges that are appropriate for them. In our own school, we have practiced flexible grouping in mathematics among all 2nd grade classes. Next, we will present an example of our way of flexible grouping.

AN EXAMPLE OF FLEXIBLE GROUPING IN GRADE 2 MATHEMATICS

In our school, we have practiced flexible grouping between grade 2 classes and the special education class. Otherwise, students have had lessons in their own classrooms, but one lesson per week has been paralleled to allow for flexible grouping. Students have been divided into three groups based on their skills: low, mid and high-achievers.

Mid and high-achievers have been working with the classroom teachers, and the low-achievers always in the special education teacher's classroom. This practice has made it possible to teach students and groups in a more individualised and targeted way. Groups are not permanent, and the students' needs for support have been assessed periodically, for example when changing topic, and groups have been modified as necessary.

Teachers have always agreed on a topic each week, and each teacher has planned their own lessons and prepared materials for them. Sometimes, lessons have been spent revising or going into more depth about the mathematical topic at hand that week, but sometimes the low-achievers' lessons, in particular, have been spent going through basics, such as sequences and the decimal system. Lower grades' and special needs materials have been used to support the learning of low-achievers, whereas the high-achievers have been directed towards problems that require in-depth mathematical thinking and problem-solving. The teachers try to include as much active learning and ICT in their teaching as feasible, for example in the form of interactive mathematical games. Students have accepted this practice quickly, and it has become a natural arrangement for them.

Often in mathematics class, either the student or the teacher checks and corrects wrong answers without analysing the answers too much. However, to support the differentiation of the student's learning and teaching, it would be more useful to ask the student to justify their answer. This can open up the student's mathematical thinking and gives the teacher precious information about how the student tries to solve the problems. Thus, the teacher can find out if the student has misunderstood something, even though the result would be correct by accident.

In the differentiation of mathematics, the assessment of the student's skills is highlighted (see Chapter 7). For example, the teacher can monitor and check some students' homework more carefully in order to get more information about what they still have to practice. In addition, one can monitor the student's learning of a certain topic through short oral testing. This way, the teacher has an easier time monitoring the student's learning and to take it into account in their own teaching.

Tips for differentiating mathematics

- Make individual progressing possible.
- Offer differentiated tasks.
- Utilise different teaching methods, such as the Varga-Neményi model.
- Use a wide variety of online activities.
- Differentiate verbal problems.
- Differentiate board work.
- Support the thought process of the student.
- Use different teaching arrangements, such as pair and group work, or flexible grouping.
- Pay attention to the assessment of the low-achievers' learning, for example by checking their homework, monitoring their class work, or by conducting short oral tests.

THE OVERALL SUPPORT OF MATHEMATICS

Low-achievers benefit from extra revision of mathematics. This can be offered to students in the form of remedial education, which can be practiced either pro-actively or reactively. One can also involve students like Catherine in remedial education in order to offer them more challenging work and mathematical problems. One should spend a lot of time on consolidating the basics in remedial education for low-achievers, because if the basics are challenging, there is no use in moving on with teaching. Especially understanding numbers, the decimal system, and different ways to break down numbers are important skills the student will stumble across and fall over in later years, if they have not understood them well enough in lower grades. By understanding numbers, we mean the names for different numbers, comparing numbers to one another, the correspondence of numbers and amounts, and categorising and organising numbers. Breaking a number down into parts, adding up to ten, and crossing the tens boundary, are skills the student will benefit from in higher grade levels. They form a basis, on which the child's later mathematical thinking and problem-solving are based. Surprisingly often, one has to return to these even in higher grade levels.

Alongside remedial education, students benefit from revising mathematics many times per day. This can be done by integrating mathematics into other subjects. For example, one can have mathematical activities in physical education. The task for the students could be to form different sized groups in which they practice division. In addition, one can practice addition, subtraction and multiplication by skipping. Addition can also be practiced by throwing balls into baskets. One can get a different number of points based on the difficulty of the shot, and the students have to count their own points. Sequences can be practiced during a game of hide-and-seek. There are many different games out there that involve mathematics, and they are easy to come up with by yourself. The most useful thing is that they help students practice the very things that are the most challenging to the low-achievers of the class.

Mathematics can be naturally integrated into crafts, through measuring, calculations or geometry. In language and literature, one can consider some verbal problems, and even come up with them for peers. Throughout the school day, one can also give low-achievers different mathematical problems related to the everyday life at school. Students can be asked to count the steps from the classroom to the cafeteria and from the classroom to the playground, and be asked to calculate the difference. Especially small students are motivated by challenges like these, and they do not always even realise that they are practising mathematics. To increase motivation, one can also use an incentive for solving a certain problem.

In the classroom, it is good to have different stimulating mathematical materials for the students to use freely. Students like to build things with different blocks or beads, which helps in developing fine motor skills and visual perception. Especially for small students, building with blocks is a fun activity that can be practiced during free time or, for example, in the end of the lesson. One should also have plenty of mathematical games available, and students can play them either during mathematics lessons or other times during the school day. Small students are particularly motivated by memory games, which can be made about multiplication or division, usually by the teacher themselves. These operations cards can be given to low-achievers to be paired up also outside of mathematics classes. In addition, different connect-the-points activities are popular among small students. They develop the learning of sequences.

Examples of overall support in mathematics

- Give low-achievers remedial education, either pro-actively or reactively.
- Focus on consolidating the basics, for example understanding numbers, the decimal system, and breaking down numbers.
- Integrate mathematics into other subjects.
- Offer a mathematically stimulating learning environment.
- Utilise different educational games.

IMAGE 7. One should consider different kinds of learners while teaching mathematics

SUPPORTING TOOLS FOR MATHEMATICS

Low-achievers in mathematics should have different support tools to help them with calculations. There are many different tools for mathematics, such as building blocks and abacuses, which can be ordered to the school. However, when the finances are tight, one can use any kinds of objects to support the students visually. For example, wooden beads or whiteboard magnets can do the job as well. A low-achiever should have their own tools, for example in their pencil case, so they can use them at home as well. A good and free tool to visualise the decimal system is an empty egg carton, which can be used to learn to cross the tens boundary through addition and subtraction. Often, students will naturally count with their fingers, which is a working practice, as they always have their fingers with them. However, it is important to teach students the clear and systematic use of their fingers, because students often use their fingers unsystematically, which can lead to mistakes.

The teacher can easily create different handouts for support. A number square with the numbers from 1 to 100 is a convenient tool to support a low-achiever's addition and subtraction. It also depicts the decimal system. Times tables on a sheet in turn help students who grapple with their multiplication. One should give the handouts individually to low-achievers, so they can glue them in their book, in order to have them available even at home. The handouts can also be attached to the top of the desk. In addition, some students can benefit from writing down the order of operations. One should also keep in mind what the topic is that is being learned during the lesson. If long division is the topic of the lesson, low-achievers should have their times tables available to be seen. Then, the full capacity of the student can be used to learn the topic at hand.

In some cases, the student can use a calculator for support. One way to differentiate mathematics is to teach a low-achiever to always check their work by using a calculator. In addition, sometimes one can agree with Rasmus or Sam that they can use a calculator for every other problem. This kind of compromise can help them work more actively.

It especially benefits low-achievers to make content concrete in their minds as much as possible. For example, a low-achiever can learn fractions much better with the use of pie models. One can come up with games with young students, in which pie models can depict a pizza or a cake, which is cut into different sized pieces. In problems with money, one can use play money to support and motivate the students better. One can also come up with role-play games in which students practice transactions and money management, while learning to count their money. These concrete support tools are useful for all students, but they can be especially used for supporting low-achievers.

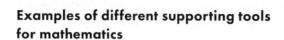

Examples of different supporting tools for mathematics

- Abacuses, blocks, magnets and wooden beads
- Number squares, sequences and times tables
- Egg cartons
- Calculators
- Legos
- Fingers

OTHER NOTABLE ISSUES

In mathematics homework, one should differentiate quantity and content. Workbooks often progress from mechanical problems in the beginning of the chapter to a few verbal application problems in the end of the chapter. Students who are a little slower often miss out on completing the verbal problems during the lesson. In some classes, if a student has not finished the chapter during the lesson, they have to finish it at home in addition to a specific homework section in the chapter. As we already noted in Chapter 5, this practice does not improve the student's motivation. Verbal problems are also included in the homework section. Thus, the student often has to complete those without the necessary support. It would be more justifiable to practice verbal application problems with the student at school, with the help of the teacher. The mechanical basic problems can be given as homework, so that the student can complete them independently. The low-achievers can be given their homework from the beginning of the chapter, so they can start to work on the application problems during the lesson. Structures in place at school, such as some scheduling choices, should not stand in the way of pedagogical choices. It is unnecessary to progress in a subject like mathematics if previous content has not been completely understood. Flexible solutions, such as individual progression for students and differentiated homework, should be encouraged better than they are now.

Despite challenges, low-achievers should be encouraged to actively and consistently practice at home at their own level. One should talk about and agree on this with the parents. The student can be given one or two problems of mathematics for homework every day, regardless of whether or not mathematics was studied that day. This kind of homework is easy to remember at home. One can also give old mathematics workbooks for the student to work through at home as extra practice. In addition, one can give operations and action cards for the student to take home, which they can complete on a few days per week alongside the homework. They usually motivate students more than their workbooks. One can agree with the student and their parents that instead of homework, the student will practice mathematics using action cards or by playing a maths game at home with their family. The important thing is that this home practice is appropriate for the student's level.

During a mathematics test, one should pay attention to differentiation. It would be optimal to give low-achievers individual tests, in which the specific content that they have learned would be measured. For example, Amy could be given a test, in which there would be more mechanical basic problems and fewer applications. One can also go through verbal problems with the low-achiever, before or after the common test situation.

Mental maths portions of the test are often done together as a whole class. However, one should also differentiate the mental maths portions of the test and offer low-achievers problems better suited to them in that regard. Students could be separated into two skill groups, and conduct the mental maths portion of the test in the beginning of the lesson with the high-achievers, and at the end with low-achievers. Alternatively, only a few students can have personalised mental maths questions. These can be gone through during a break, before the test or after it.

One should also differentiate the time that is spent on the test based on the skills of the students, because some students need more time than the duration of one lesson to complete a mathematics test. In addition to students like Amy, this practice also benefits students with trouble concentrating. We have experience of students like Rasmus or Sam, who have completed a mathematics test in small hurdles, even across three days, because of their problems with concentration.

As in all learning, the support of the home is highlighted in mathematics, especially with the situation of a low-achiever. One should tell the parents about the different ways they can support their children's mathematical skills at home. One can also give them tips to support the student's practice in mathematics. For example, one can ask the parents to glue times tables around the bathroom mirror, so the student can practice them while brushing their teeth. The student can also be encouraged to play mathematical games, because it is beneficial and often motivating. In addition, the student can be directed to count and compare different objects. This way, mathematics will be better understood by the child.

In this chapter, we highlighted some of the integral principles and practices to differentiating mathematics instruction. In addition to the things we discussed, differentiation according to the 5D model shown in Part III of the book is highlighted in mathematics. For example, it is useful to utilise different teaching arrangements shown in Chapter 3, such as co-teaching, learning assistants and parallel lessons.

Tips to remedy the starting point

GRADE 1: SAM

- Use activities in mathematics, such as operation and action cards.
- Differentiate in the number of problems, not the difficulty.
- Use ICT, such as different games and e-learning problems.
- Motivate to count using different supporting materials, such as blocks and a calculator.
- Involve parents to support mathematics.

GRADE 3: RASMUS

- Use ICT, such as different games and e-learning problems.
- Differentiate in the number of problems, not the difficulty.
- Try contractual project work in mathematics.
- Make it possible to complete the test in parts.

GRADE 5: AMY

– Offer many concrete tools to support calculations, such as blocks, an abacus, pie models or a number square.

– Utilise peer support.

– Differentiate in the number and difficulty of problems, and if necessary, offer individualised problems.

– Focus on consolidating the basics.

– Differentiate the content and time spent on the mathematics test.

– Support verbal problems at school and assign mechanical basic problems as homework.

GRADE 9: CATHERINE

– Offer challenging extra problems. Utilise materials from upper grade levels.

– Give remedial education, if possible.

– Provide more challenging homework.

– Group students flexibly based on learning profiles, and offer targeted teaching for high-achievers.

10. FOREIGN LANGUAGES

The starting point

GRADE 5: AMY

Amy has studied French for over two years now. First, she was excited about learning a foreign language, but learning French proved to be challenging very quickly, which killed her enthusiasm. Amy now finds learning foreign languages unpleasant, and she gets anxious even thinking about French lessons. Her dyslexia makes it difficult for her to learn French. It is hard to learn new things, and she has to work a lot to understand unfamiliar sounds. Amy feels that the teaching is too difficult for her, and she often feels like she does not understand anything during lessons. She follows what others do and copies them. Speaking publicly in French classed makes Amy especially nervous. She completes her homework as well as she can and tries to study for the test, but she feels like she simply cannot remember the vocabulary. In a test situation, Amy feels that she runs out of time. She is worried about it beforehand, and she rushes the test in order to complete it in time.

GRADE 9: CATHERINE

Catherine is talented in German. She has a wide vocabulary and she can read, speak and write German excellently for her age. There are always some new words in the chapters the class listens to in lessons, but she learns them quickly. She completes the exercises in class quickly, and would like to carry on, but is prohibited by the teacher to do so. Catherine can complete listening comprehension exercises on the first go, and she has to sit and wait for others to listen to the exercises for multiple times. She is assigned the same homework as others, and she completes them quickly and effortlessly. Lately, Catherine has not completed all of her homework, because she does not find it motivating or necessary.

Many students find foreign languages difficult. Dyslexia in particular can make learning foreign languages challenging for students, but even they who have mastered their own mother tongue can have trouble learning a new language. So far, learning difficulties in foreign languages has not been thoroughly researched. Nonetheless, this is an important topic as modern society has seen multilingualism become a norm, and the European commission recommends that every European should command two other languages in addition to their mother tongue (European Commission 1995). Consequently, it is important that those with learning difficulties who are learning foreign languages are supported, for example, through differentiation.

In this chapter, we will explore differentiation in four areas of learning a language: listening comprehension, speaking, reading comprehension and writing. In the end, we will consider some general issues related to differentiating the teaching of foreign languages.

LISTENING COMPREHENSION

In foreign language teaching, students hear a lot of the foreign language. Often, the teacher gives instructions in the language, and students listen to different kinds of recordings during lessons. Thus, in a lesson, one gets a lot of auditive information, which one must understand in order to act in a certain way. However, for many students like Amy, understanding speech in a foreign language is difficult.

IMAGE 8. In foreign language class, the most important instructions should be given simply and with support

While starting the lessons, one should make the student's ears ready to receive information in a foreign language. For small children, this can be done through a game or a song. Common routines, such as greetings, which are repeated in every lesson, are a good way to activate the student's perception of foreign language.

In lessons, the teacher should concentrate on their own speech. It is good to change the tone, difficulty and variety in one's language depending on to whom one is speaking. A way to differentiate this is to first introduce the topic using more complex sentence structures, which serves high-achievers like Catherine, and after this, introduce the same topic in simpler terms. Overall, one should repeat oneself often when teaching in a foreign language, and paraphrase everything one says, so that everyone understands. This way, low-achievers will understand better, and high-achievers can learn multiple ways to express the same thing. For example, when asking about the students' favourite foods in Spanish, one can use different questions: '¿Cuál es tu comida favorita?', or '¿Qué te gusta comer?'. One can also support one's speech in many ways. For example, pictures, gestures and expressions can help the lowest achievers understand what the teacher is talking about. Important or difficult words can also be described or translated, or have another student translate them for the rest of the class, so that everyone understands them.

In foreign language lessons, listening comprehension exercises are done often, and they can be very difficult for many students. One can use many methods to consider students of different skill levels during listening comprehension exercises. Often the listening exercise is listened to only a few times, so that a low-achiever does not have enough time to quite understand what is being said. It is important to let a student listen to the text multiple times. Nowadays, almost all classrooms have computers in them. Thus, some students can be let to listen to the exercise multiple times, for example with headphones. Meanwhile, other students can do other work. One should also divide the listening comprehension exercise into smaller pieces, so that low-achievers can pick out the most important bits of what they hear. One can also offer a vocabulary list to support the student's listening. In addition, sometimes it is justified to give the student the whole text, so that they can follow it during the listening exercise.

Overall, it is important to be pre-emptive when working with a low-achiever. Some students can be told beforehand about the topic and central content of the listening comprehension exercise. This will make it easier for them to understand and work through the anxiety-inducing situation. One can also give the text to the student in need of support for them to take it home. This gives them an opportunity to familiarise themselves with the content prior to the lesson. One can also give the student a vocabulary list of words most important to understanding the text.

It is also justified to differentiate answering listening comprehension exercises. Low-achievers should get an opportunity to answer structured yes or no questions, whereas high-achievers can be offered more variable and detailed exercises. The questions can be read and translated for some of the group beforehand, while others work on something else. An effortless practice to differentiate is to ask high-achievers to write words and sentences present in the exercise in their notebooks. It is important to consider the students' self-confidence and motivation. An experience of understanding and making sense of the recording creates a positive feeling and faith in one's own learning.

Tips to differentiate listening comprehension

- Pre-empt and verbalise exercises and actions.
- Let the student familiarise themselves with the text or topic pre-emptively, using remedial education or homework.
- Vary your speech. Use repetition and paraphrasing.
- Support speech with pictures, gestures and expressions.
- Describe or translate important words.
- Let the student listen to the exercise recording many times, and break the exercises down into many smaller parts.
- Offer vocabulary lists to the student for support.
- Offer the student a written version of the spoken text.
- Use different exercise types.

SPEAKING

Speaking a foreign language is a scary and challenging situation for many students. Research shows that many students are nervous about speaking foreign languages, and are scared about others laughing at their speaking skills (Pihko 2007). Because of this, one should encourage and positively acknowledge the students' verbal products, no matter how small. One should give an opportunity for low-achievers in speaking to give their answers in one word. However, one can expect high-achievers like Catherine to answer in complete and more complex sentences. One way is to enable the participation of low-achievers by letting them answer in the common language of instruction. For many students, it is already hard to understand the questions in a foreign language, so an answer in the common language of instruction can be completely justified. One can also give vocabulary words or model sentences to low-achievers to support them in speaking exercises.

Pair and group work are well-suited for differentiating speech exercises in a foreign language. Students find them safer than speaking in front of the whole class. Then, even the low-achievers can be encouraged to use the foreign language, even if it is only a little. In addition to this, the lowest achievers can be given pre-written model conversation to support their conversation with a partner or group. Sometimes, the teacher can be the partner of a low-achiever during a conversation exercise, so that the student does not have to be nervous about the others' reactions. One can differentiate the speech of high-achievers by grouping them together, or by the teacher having a conversation with them about different topics.

If the student gets nervous about speaking in a foreign language, they can be given a chance to record their speech at home. This recording can then be brought to school for the teacher to listen to. This can alleviate the pressure a student feels about talking, and they have the opportunity to record and re-record as many times as they need. One can also have the students practice talking in class or reading out loud by asking the students to read or speak to themselves, out loud, but mumbling under their breath. A single student's voice or pronunciation will not stand out, but the teacher can go around the classroom to listen to each student and give them direction.

Some students have a hard time with the motor skills of their tongue while speaking in a foreign language. One can use a mirror to support learning some sounds. The students can look at their tongue and how it is positioned, for example when rolling their 'r's. In addition, to practice the 'p' sound in many languages, one can keep their hand in front of their mouth and teach students that, for example in Spanish, there should be very little air coming out of their mouth during 'p' sounds, as opposed to English, when one should feel the air on their palm.

Tips to differentiate speech

- Use flexible grouping.
- Give positive feedback for all effort.
- Give an opportunity to have short conversations or to give single word answers.
- Allow for answers in the common language of instruction (or mother tongue when applicable) in conversation exercises.
- Offer vocabulary lists and pre-written model sentences to support speaking exercises.
- Use group and pair discussions, talking to oneself, and mumbling.
- Use pre-written model conversations in conversation exercises.
- Allow for conversations with the teacher and recording speech.
- Teach to use a mirror to practice speech.

READING COMPREHENSION

Differentiation entails that everyone does not have to study exactly same things at the same time. This principle works well in the differentiation of reading comprehension in foreign language lessons. For example, the chapters of textbooks are often too long and challenging for students like Amy, so they have a hard time following the text and picking out the most important information. Instead of textbook readings, these students could be given individualised texts, which are appropriate for their skill levels. One can come up with exercises related to the texts, which do not take much time or effort from the teacher to prepare ahead of time, for example: 'What do you think are the three most important things in the text? Translate these either orally or in writing.'

According to the idea of effective differentiation, one can utilise the student's areas of interest in choosing texts for them to read. This increases their commitment to learning. Students can bring their own texts to class, such as lyrics to a song. These can be used as learning materials during the lesson. One should direct high-achievers like Catherine to read challenging texts in a foreign language. The student can, for example, have a book written in a foreign language in their desk, which they can read when they have completed other tasks.

Often, it is completely justified and practical to use the same text with the whole class. Then, the text should be modified and made simpler for low-achievers to use. One can shorten the texts by cutting out sentences not completely necessary for the progression of the text, and only leave the content necessary for the student to understand. For example, one can strike out the unnecessary sentences from the student's textbook. This task could be given to a high-achiever in lower secondary school as an differentiative activity.

Wide-ranging and detailed texts can be differentiated by replacing difficult words with easier synonyms, or by shortening sentences by removing extra words or unnecessary subordinate clauses. In addition, one can underline the most important words or write them in italics or bold. One can also translate the most difficult concepts. One should also pay attention to the format of the text, in order to support the understanding and perception of the students. For example, clear paragraphs, sub-titles and the use of illustrations and pictures can help with reading comprehension. Teaching reading strategies to the students is highlighted in differentiating reading in a foreign language. For example, going over the titles and pictures of the text helps students understand the most important things.

In conclusion, there are many ways in which one can differentiate reading comprehension exercises in foreign language teaching. Through these methods, one can better take different learners into consideration. Using modern technology, copying and editing the textbook chapter is very easy, and it does not take an obscene amount of time. In addition, one can use simplified texts in later years with new students, or during the next lesson while going through homework. Carefully prepared, differentiated texts serve teaching even in the future, and save time taken to differentiate. One should consider the so-called affective factors again. It is important in terms of motivation and self-confidence that every student gets the feeling that they have the skills to read a text in a foreign language.

Tips to differentiate reading comprehension

- Familiarise the student with the text prior to the lesson, for instance in remedial education or as homework.
- Offer individualised texts to the students.
- Utilise the students' own texts.
- Use simplified texts.
- Replace hard words with easier synonyms.
- Shorten the sentences in the text.
- Edit the format of the text so that you use clear paragraphs, sub-titles and supportive pictures.
- Teach the students reading strategies.

WRITING

Although the main objective in modern foreign language teaching should be oral output, writing is also an important part of knowing a foreign language. This is especially practiced in higher grade levels. However, writing is very hard for some students, especially due to spelling rules and the fact that, in many languages, words are not written the same way as they are pronounced.

One should approach writing individually and by putting the students first. Some written exercises are better suited for differentiation than others. An example of this is different projects and presentations, which everyone can complete based on their skills and capacities. Thus, they naturally differentiate learning for both low and high-achievers. For example, while writing about their favourite hobbies, high-achievers like Catherine can produce long texts, in which there are hard vocabulary and challenging structures, whereas students like Amy can only list single words related to the hobby.

One should start differentiation from the very topic of the exercise. The students are more motivated and committed to the writing exercise if they can choose their topic by themselves. One way to differentiate and challenge high-achievers is to ask them to keep a journal in the foreign language. This can be their homework, instead of regular exercises. The student can occasionally bring their journal to school for the teacher to read and check.

Often, some form of written exercise is necessary for younger students as well. However, one should consider the differences of each student when assessing written work as the students are only practising their writing. In addition, it is good to keep in mind that the main emphasis in foreign language teaching in lower grades is on spoken language. When expecting perfect grammar from a young student, one is not considering students with dyslexia, who struggle with letters even in their first language. Thus, one can justifiably accept misspelt words and missed letters.

Lowest achievers can only complete the easiest exercises from the workbook, and it is often wise to only have them complete some of the hard or long exercises. Especially when differentiating writing, one should utilise materials from lower grade levels, because book series often use similar themes each year, such as animals or hobbies. For open-ended questions, low-achievers can give one-word answers instead of full sentences. Furthermore, one can assign only the most important words in the vocabulary as homework.

Computers are a good tool for differentiating writing in a foreign language. In most word-processing programmes, one can select different languages for the spell-checker, which reveals typing errors and directs the student to produce words correctly. In addition, there are many online exercises at different levels about many themes and grammar structures that can be used to differentiate. Using a computer also serves those students who have challenges in fine motor skills and using a pencil.

Tips to differentiate writing

- Use differentiated exercises, such as projects.
- Accept answering with single words instead of answering in full sentences.
- Utilise the student's own areas of interest.
- Give positive feedback for all effort.
- Do not pick on single spelling errors.
- Allow the students to use their first language based on their individual goals.
- Utilise learning materials and writing exercises from lower grade levels.
- Use a computer to support correct spelling.

OTHER NOTABLE ISSUES

In addition to what has been presented above, one can use many general methods to differentiate teaching foreign languages. For example, one should pay attention to differentiating homework. Often, each student is assigned the same homework. However, high-achievers may only take a few minutes to complete the homework, whereas a low-achiever can spend tens of minutes with the same task. Thus, it is often justified to give fewer and less complicated tasks for low-achievers as homework. For example, students like Amy can have homework that emphasise oral exercises and practising vocabulary. We have explored this topic more broadly in Chapter 5.

Test conditions are another integral part of the differentiation of foreign language teaching. When the teacher is aware of the students' level of proficiency, there is not necessarily a need to have a test. Instead, capabilities can be proven by a portfolio or even a video. If the teacher still uses a test to support the measurement of the student reaching their learning goals, one should pay attention to time during the test. We all have our individual rate at which we work, and some need a little more time than others to complete a certain task. Sometimes, a teacher expects everyone to finish the test during one lesson. This in itself is a source of anxiety when it comes to taking a test, and has a negative effect on the test result. It is imperative that some students can complete their test in parts and that they know and understand this. In addition, it is useful for many students to only give them the test one question at a time, instead of slamming the whole test in front of them at once. Knowing one's students is, once again, highlighted here; some students, like Amy, truly need more time for a test, while others can complete the whole test during one lesson.

While drafting the test, one should think whether some students might benefit from a slightly easier test, which has more word recognition exercises than exercises that require the student to produce text. In addition, the student should be given the opportunity to give their answers orally, either for some or the whole of the test. One should also consider whether some students could be accepted to give a misspelt answer if the answer resembles the pronounced form of the word (for example *bone joor* vs. *bonjour*). Vocabulary tests can also be held orally, either with the whole class, or individually with a single student.

Remedial education is also a good way to differentiate the student's learning in foreign languages. It can be done pro-actively, so that one pre-emptively goes through the next chapter of the text book or the next grammar structure that will be taught with the low-achiever. Alternatively, one can give reactive remedial education, in which the teacher goes through what has already been taught so the student can revise the content.

It also makes differentiation easier if the school has resources to use a learning assistant or co-teaching. With these, one can flexibly group students based on different factors and offer the groups targeted teaching. In addition, it would be beneficial to have a special education needs resource available for foreign language teaching. Paralleling lessons even across grade levels enables co-teaching, and one can also parallel the lesson with a special education lesson to make use of that resource. The student can also take part in a lesson at a lower or higher grade level. These arrangements have been explored in more detail in Chapter 3.

Tips to remedy the starting point

GRADE 5: AMY

- Use proactive remedial education.
- Assign individualised homework.
- Give extra time for completing a test or let complete the test orally.
- Use easier tests.
- Accept pronounced spelling (i.e. *bone joor* vs. *bonjour*).
- Use plain language texts.
- Utilise a computer.
- Offer an opportunity to listen to the chapters of the textbook at home.
- Explain the topic of the lesson pre-emptively in the common language of instruction.
- Differentiate speech exercises by letting her pair up with the teacher or record speech at home.
- Use pair or group support.
- Use a learning assistant.

GRADE 9: CATHERINE

- Differentiate listening comprehension exercises, for example by expecting answers in full sentences.
- Direct towards writing projects and in-depth presentations.
- Direct to write a journal in the foreign language.
- Assign more challenging homework. Utilise materials from higher grade levels.
- Have conversations with the student in the foreign language.

AFTERWORD

Although differentiation does not make miracles happen, with it, one can offer each student meaningful learning experiences. In this book, we have defined differentiation both as a way to approach teaching and as a bundle of methods to take each student's individuality into account. The goal of the book has been to implement differentiation as a working part of teaching culture and the everyday life of the teacher.

Optimal differentiation requires a certain attitude adjustment. Instead of traditional education, one should create a culture in the classroom that is more flexible and where not all students have to work on the same tasks in the same way or at the same time. As we have stated multiple times in this book, differentiation can be started small, for example by only differentiating one dimension of teaching or one subject.

We hope that this book has made you, as the reader, convinced about the importance of differentiation and offered an abundance of tips to practice differentiation. Although the emphasis has been on differentiating to support low-achievers, we have, throughout the book, tried to highlight the importance of differentiation for everyone, even for high-achievers. Even though we have explored many different differentiation practices in the book, there are many left unexplored. We wish that, once they have read this book, the teacher could reflect on their own teaching from the perspective of differentiation, thus finding appropriate solutions and practices for each student in different situations.

When differentiation has been successful, the education of our example students looks like this:

GRADE 1: SAM

Sam's education has been widely differentiated throughout the school year in many dimensions. First, the teacher started to only give him very short work times, which have then slowly been extended. The teacher has also varied Sam's learning activities during the lesson, and Sam has had the opportunity to practice with a computer or educational game towards the end of the lesson. This has motivated Sam to work more effectively. Gradually, the time Sam spends on work effectively has increased from five to 30 minutes. Occasionally, he has been able to work for a whole

lesson. Differentiating Sam's homework has started to prove to be worthwhile too. Reducing the amount of homework and making it more individualised, as well as letting him have a say in the content of the homework has made him more committed to completing it. Of course, sometimes he still forgets to do them, but considerably less than in the beginning of the year. Due to differentiation, Sam has learned the main goals of the first grade and has learned to read and write at beginner level.

Differentiating the learning environment has had a positive effect on Sam's education. Sam's desk is at the back of the classroom and he sometimes uses a partition to help him concentrate. The teacher has agreed on a practice that allows Sam to get up from his desk to walk around, and he can also move around in the corridor a few times during the lesson. This has reduced Sam's disruptive behaviour during lessons. He no longer bothers others during the lessons anymore, even towards the end of the lesson, but reads, draws or plays something by himself. Overall, differentiation has motivated Sam, and he has begun to get more interested in school. The teacher has been less tired, and their communication with the home has become better, as they have been able to send positive notes to Sam's home.

GRADE 3: RASMUS

The teacher has differentiated Rasmus' education, both in classroom work and free time. He has had added support during breaks. In the beginning of the school year, Rasmus always spent breaks with a teacher or learning assistant. Towards the end of the autumn semester, older peer mentors have joined breaks to arrange games for younger students. Sometimes, Rasmus still spends his break indoors with a few peers, especially when he feels tired. Rasmus has made some friends in the class, and this has clearly reduced the number of conflicts at school. Rasmus' studying has been differentiated through contractual project work. Rasmus has received a task list in the beginning of the lesson, and later in the beginning of the school day. Once he has completed the tasks, he has been allowed to draw or do something else he likes. In addition, the teacher has agreed with Rasmus that if he has completed his homework properly in the beginning of the week, he does not get homework for the last two days. These practices have motivated Rasmus to work considerably better in the classroom.

The teacher has also used a systematic incentive practice, which has encouraged Rasmus to try his best at school. He receives a sticker for a good day and five stickers leads to a prize agreed on with his parents. This has clearly improved his behaviour and reduced his tendency to laugh at or comment on others' answers in class. Overall, differentiation has had a positive effect on Rasmus' learning and on the learning environment of the whole class.

GRADE 5: AMY

The teacher has differentiated Amy's education by reducing the number of topics covered and by making the content easier. In teaching, the teacher has focused on the core contents with Amy, which has enabled her to reach the main objectives at her grade level. The grade 5 teachers have used flexible grouping in mathematics teaching, and occasionally in other subjects. This has had a positive effect on Amy's learning and her social relationships. Amy has also received some remedial education from the special education teacher.

Through differentiation, Amy has learned the core content in different subjects. Her homework has been reduced and assigned individually. Amy has learned to use a homework notebook, through which her parents have been able to support her with homework, and the teacher has not had to send them a message about individual homework each time. Amy has also used plain text and audio book versions of the textbooks in many subjects, which has helped her understand the content. In addition, Amy has practiced foreign languages with flash cards and partially completed her tests orally. In written work, the teacher has not demanded perfect spelling, if the word has been recognisable. Because of this, Amy has gotten experiences of success even during tests, which has helped to create a more positive attitude towards the foreign language. The teacher has also utilised peer support with Amy, using pair and group work, and taught her individualised studying strategies and the use of ICT in studying. Overall, differentiated instruction has offered Amy positive learning experiences, and above all, it has improved her self-confidence as a learner.

GRADE 9: CATHERINE

During the school year, teachers have begun to differentiate Catherine's studying. Where Catherine used to draw or daydream during the end of the lesson, teachers have now directed her towards more in-depth study. For example, Catherine has used an upper secondary school level books in mathematics alongside the one for her grade level. She has worked on that at the end of the lesson. In Catherine's school, teachers have started to collaborate, and for example, the history and German teachers have asked Catherine to complete a project, in which she has studied an important historical period and created an end product in German. She has worked on this at home, and at the end of history and German lessons. Furthermore, teachers have contacted the local upper secondary school to see if Catherine could take part in some of their German lessons.

Catherine still finishes all her work during the lesson, and gets by without doing much homework. However, under the instruction of her language and literature teacher, she has written a learning journal at home, in which she has reflected on things she has learned at school each day. This has taught Catherine to work hard towards her education. Differentiation has provided Catherine with appropriate challenges. When she has had an opportunity to study at her own level and with content that interests her, education feels meaningful again. Catherine has learned to put in effort again, as things that are taught to her are not completely self-evident.

REFERENCES

Ahtiainen, R., Beirad, M., Hautamäki, J., Hilasvuori, T. & Thuneberg, H. 2011. *Samanaikaisopetus on mahdollisuus. Tutkimus Helsingin pilottikoulujen uudistuvasta opetuksesta.* (Publication A1 by Helsinki Department of Education).

Ashcraft, M. H., Krause, J. A. & Hopko, D. R. 2007. Is math anxiety a mathematical learning disability? In D. B. Berch & M. M. M. Mazzocco (eds.) *Why is math so hard for some children? The nature and origins of mathematical learning difficulties and disabilities.* Baltimore: Paul H. Brookes, 329–348.

Aunio, P. 2014. Miksi lapsi ei opi laskemaan? *EriKa – Erityispedagoginen tutkimus- ja menetelmätieto* 1, 30–34.

Baker, S., Gersten, R. & Lee, D.-S. 2002. A synthesis of empirical research on teaching mathematics to low-achieving students. *The Elementary School Journal* 103 (1), 51–73.

Berbaum, K. A. 2009. *Initiating differentiated instruction in general education classrooms with inclusion learning support students: a multiple case study.* Walden University.

DeBaryshe, B. D., Gorecki, D. M. & Mishima-Young, L. N. 2009. Differentiated instruction to support high-risk preschool learners. *NHSA Dialog* 2 (3), 227–244.

Dörnyei, Z. & Ushioda, E. 2013. *Teaching and researching motivation.* 2nd ed. New York: Routledge.

Ekonoja, A. 2014. *Oppimateriaalien kehittäminen, hyödyntäminen ja rooli tieto- ja viestintätekniikan opetuksessa.* Jyväskylä Studies in Computing 193.

European Commission. 1995. *White paper on education and training. Teaching and learning: towards the learning society.* <http://europa.eu/documents/comm/white_pa- pers/pdf/com95_590_en.pdf> (Accessed 26.2.2017).

Fischer, K. W. & Rose, L. T. 2001. Webs of skill: How students learn. *Educational Leadership* 59 (3), 6–12.

FNCCBE = Finnish National Core Curriculum for Basic Education. 2014. 4th ed. Helsinki: Finnish National Board of Education

Frønes, I. 2016. The absence of failure: Children at risk in the knowledge based economy. *Child Indicators Research* 9 (1), 247–260.

Fuchs, L. S., Compton, D. L., Fuchs, D., Paulsen, K., Bryant, J. D. & Hamlett, C. L. 2005. The prevention, identification, and cognitive determinants of math difficulty. *Journal of Educational Psychology* 97 (3), 493–513.

Gardner, H. 2008. *Multiple intelligences. New horizons.* New York: Basic Books.

Gauffin, K., Vinnerljung, B., Fridell, M., Hesse, M. & Hjern, A. 2013. Childhood socio-economic status, school failure and drug abuse: A Swedish national cohort study. *Addiction* 108 (8), 1441–1449.

Goodley, D. 2001. "Learning difficulties", the social model of disability and impairment: Challenging epistemologies. *Disability & Society* 16 (2), 207–231.

Grigorenko, E. L., Jarvin, L. & Sternberg, R. J. 2002. School-based tests of the triarchic theory of intelligence: Three settings, three samples, three syllabi. *Contemporary Educational Psychology* 27 (2), 167–208.

Hayward, L. 2012. Assessment and learning: The learner's perspective. In J. Gardner (ed.) *Assessment and Learning.* 2nd ed. London: Sage, 125–139.

Hodgson, P. & Pang, M. Y. C. 2012. Effective formative e-assessment of student learning: A study on a statistics course. *Assessment & Evaluation in Higher Education* 37 (2), 215–225.

Itkonen, T., Dervin, F. & Talib, M. T. 2017. Finnish education: An ambiguous utopia? *International Journal of Bias, Identity and Diversities in Education (IJBIDE)* 2 (2), 13–28.

Kanevsky, L. & Keighley, T. 2003. To produce or not to produce? Understanding boredom and the honor in underachievement. *Roeper Review* 26 (1), 20–28.

Karadag, R. & Yasar, S. 2010. Effects of differentiated instruction on students' attitudes towards Turkish courses: An action research. *Procedia – Social and Behavioral Sciences* 9, 1394–1399.

Keltikangas-Järvinen, L. 2006. *Hyvä itsetunto.* 17th ed. Helsinki: WSOY.

Koeze, P. A. 2007. Differentiated instruction: The effect on student achievement in an elementary school. *Masters Theses and Doctoral Dissertations.* Paper 31.

Koivula, P. 2012. *Kolmiportainen tuki ja pidennetty oppivelvollisuus uusien normien mukaan – mitä lausuntojen kirjoittajien ja erityisen tuen päätöksen tekijöiden tulisi tietää.* Helsinki: Finnish Ministry of Education. <http://www.oph. /download/144777_Koi- vula_Oppilashuollon_paivat.pdf> (Accessed 24.2.2017).

Kulik, J. A. & Kulik, C.-L. C. 1992. Meta-analytic findings on grouping programs. *Gifted Child Quarterly* 36 (2), 73–77.

Kupiainen, S., Hautamäki, J. & Karjalainen, T. 2009. *The Finnish education system and PISA.* Helsinki: Ministry of Education.

Lakkala, S. 2008. *Inklusiivinen opettajuus. Toimintatutkimus opettajankoulutuksessa.* Lapin yliopisto. Acta Universitatis Lapponiensis 151.

Lämsä, T. & Erkolahti, R. 2013. Valikoiva puhumattomuus – haasteena lapsen vaikeneminen. *Duodecim* 129 (24), 2641–2646.

McCrea Simpkins, P., Mastropieri, M. A. & Scruggs, T. E. 2009. Differentiated curriculum enhancements in inclusive fifth-grade science classes. *Remedial and Special Education* 30 (5), 300–308.

McNamara, J. K., Willoughby, T. & Chalmers, H. 2005. Psychosocial status of adolescents with learning disabilities with and without comorbid attention deficit hyperactivity disorder. *Learning Disabilities Research & Practice* 20 (4), 234–244.

McNulty, M. A. 2003. Dyslexia and the life course. *Journal of Learning Disabilities* 36 (4), 363–381.

McTighe, J. & Brown, J. L. 2005. Differentiated instruction and educational standards: Is détente possible? *Theory Into Practice* 44 (3), 234–244.

Mikola, M. 2011. *Pedagogista rajankäyntiä koulussa. Inkluusioreitit ja yhdessä oppimisen edellytykset.* Jyväskylä Studies in Education, Psychology and Social Research 412.

Miles, S. B. & Stipek, D. 2006. Contemporaneous and longitudinal associations between social behavior and literacy achievement in a sample of low-income elementary school children. *Child Development* 77 (1), 103–117.

Ministry of Education. 2008. *Education and science in Finland.* Helsinki: Ministry of Education publications 25.

Ministry of Education and Culture. 2019. *Education system in Finland.* https://minedu.fi/documents/1410845/15514014/Education+system+in+Finland/7c5a920b-47a5-c3ce-cbca-818ff3a5f848/Education+system+in+Finland.pdf

Mononen, R., Aunio, P., Väisänen, E., Korhonen, J. & Tapola, A. 2017. *Matemaattiset oppimisvaikeudet.* Jyväskylä: PS-kustannus.

Nakamura, J. & Csikszentmihalyi, M. 2009. Flow theory and research. In S. J. Lopez & C. R. Snyder (eds.) *The Oxford Handbook of Positive Psychology.* 2nd ed. Oxford: Oxford University Press, 195–206.

Naukkarinen, A. 2005. *Osallistavaa koulua rakentamassa. Tutkimus yleisopetuksen koulun ja erityiskoulun yhdistymisen prosessista.* Helsinki: The Finnish Ministry of Education.

OECD. 2003. *Literacy Skills for the World of Tomorrow.* Further results from PISA 2000. http://www.oecd.org/edu/school/2960581.pdf

OECD. 2004. *First results from PISA 2003. Executive Summary.* http://www.oecd.org/edu/school/programmeforinternationalstudentassessmentpisa/34002454.pdf

OECD. 2007. *PISA 2006 results. Executive summary.* http://www.oecd.org/pisa/pisaproducts/39725224.pdf

OECD. 2010. *PISA 2009 Results: Executive Summary.* http://www.oecd.org/pisa/pisaproducts/46619703.pdf

OECD. 2014. *PISA 2012 Results in Focus. What 15-year-olds know and what they can do with what they know?* http://www.oecd.org/pisa/keyfindings/pisa-2012-results-overview.pdf

OECD. 2018. *PISA 2015 Results in Focus.* https://www.oecd.org/pisa/pisa-2015-results-in-focus.pdf

Oliver, M. 1996. *Understanding disability: from theory to practice.* New York: St Martin's Press.

OSF = Official Statistics of Finland. 2018a. *Pre-primary and comprehensive school education* (e-publication). Helsinki: Statistics Finland. https://www.stat.fi/til/pop/2018/pop_2018_2018-11-14_tie_001_en.html

OSF = Official Statistics of Finland. 2018b. *Special education* (e-publication). Helsinki: Statistics Finland. http://www.stat.fi/til/erop/2014/erop_2014_2015-06-11_tie_001_en.html

Perusopetus [Basic Education]. (n.d.). https://www.oph.fi/koulutus_ja_tutkinnot/perusopetus

Pihko, M. K. 2007. Minä, koulu ja englanti. Vertaileva tutkimus englanninkielisen sisällönopetuksen ja perinteisen englannin opetuksen affektiivisista tuloksista. Jyväskylä: University of Jyväskylä. Department of Teacher Education, Research Report 85.

Pulkkinen, J. & Rytivaara, A. 2010. Yhteistyö, samanaikaisopettaminen ja eriyttäminen – Lecture.

Rauste-von Wright, M., von Wright, J. & Soini, T. 2003. *Oppiminen ja koulutus.* Helsinki: WSOY.

Reis, S. M., McCoach, D. B., Little, C. A., Muller, L. M. & Kaniskan, R. B. 2011. The effects of differentiated instruction and enrichment pedagogy on reading achievement in five elementary schools. *American Educational Research Journal* 48 (2), 462–501.

Roiha, A. 2014. Teachers' views on differentiation in content and language integrated learning (CLIL): Perceptions, practices and challenges. *Language and Education* 28 (1), 1–18.

Räsänen, P. 2012. Laskemiskyvyn häiriö eli dyskalkulia. *Duodecim* 128 (11), 1168–1177.

Sahlberg, P. 2011. *Finnish lessons. What can the world learn from educational change in Finland?* New York: Teachers College Press.

Seppälä, R. & Kautto-Knape, E. 2009. Eriyttämisen tavat englannin opetuksessa. *Kielikukko* 28 (4), 13–18.

Shaunessy-Dedrick, E., Evans, L., Ferron, J. & Lindo, M. 2015. Effects of differentiated reading on elementary students' reading comprehension and attitudes toward reading. *Gifted Child Quarterly* 59 (2), 91–107.

Sideridis, G. D. 2003. On the origins of helpless behavior of students with learning disabilities: Avoidance motivation? *International Journal of Educational Research* 39 (4–5), 497–517.

Sousa, D. & Tomlinson, C. A. 2011. *Differentiation and brain: How neuroscience supports the learner-friendly classroom.* Bloomington, IN: Solution Tree.

Subban, P. 2006. Differentiated instruction: A research basis. *International Education Journal* 7 (7), 935–947.

Thousand, J. S. & Villa, R. A. & Nevin, A. I. 2006. The many faces of collaborative planning and teaching. *Theory into Practice* 45 (3), 239–248.

Thousand, J. S., Villa, R. A. & Nevin, A. I. 2007. *Differentiating instruction: Collaborative planning and teaching for universally designed learning.* Thousand Oaks, CA: Corwin Press.

Tieso, C. L. 2003. Ability grouping is not just tracking anymore. *Roeper Review* 26 (1), 29–36.

Toivonen, S. 2014. *Matkalla kohti digikoulua.* Helsinki: SanomaPro. <https:// www. sanomapro. /opetus-ja-opiskelu/matkalla-kohti-digikoulua> (Accessed 23.1.2017).

Tomlinson, C. A. 2001. *How to differentiate instruction in mixed-ability classrooms.* 2nd ed. Alexandria: ASCD.

Tomlinson, C. A. 2004. *Fulfilling the promise of the differentiated classroom: Strategies and tools for responsive teaching.* Alexandria: ASCD.

Tomlinson, C. A. 2005. Grading and differentiation: Paradox or good practice? *Theory into Practice* 44 (3), 262–269.

Tomlinson, C. A. 2014. *The differentiated classroom: responding to the needs of all learners.* 2nd ed. Alexandria: ASCD.

Tomlinson, C. A., Brighton, C., Hertberg, H., Callahan, C. M., Moon, K. B., Conover, L. A. & Reynolds, T. 2003. Differentiating instruction in response to student readiness, interest, and learning profile in academically diverse classrooms: A review of literature. *Journal for the Education of the Gifted* 27 (2–3), 119–145.

Tomlinson, C. A., Brimijoin, K. & Narvaez, L. 2008. *The differentiated school. Making revolutionary changes in teaching and learning.* Alexandria: ASCD.

Tomlinson, C. A. & Imbeau, M. B. 2010. *Leading and managing a differentiated classroom.* Alexandria: ASCD.

Trzesniewski, K., Moffit, T. E., Caspi, A., Taylor, A. & Maughan, B. 2006. Revisiting the association between reading achievement and antisocial behavior: New evidence of an environmental explanation from a twin study. *Child Development* 77 (1), 72–88.

Tynjälä, P. 1999. *Oppiminen tiedon rakentamisena. Konstruktivistisen oppimiskäsityksen perusteita* Helsinki: Kirjayhtymä.

Virtanen, H. 2014. *Selkokielen tarvearvio 2014* (Selkokeskus, The Finnish Association on Intellectual and Developmental Disabilities). <http:// selkokeskus.fi/wordpress/wp-content/uploads/2016/05/Tarvearvio_2014_ kevyt.pdf> (Accessed 4.7.2017).

Vygotsky, L. S. 1978. *Mind in society. The development of higher psychological processes.* Eds. M. Cole, V. John-Steiner, S. Scribner & E. Souberman. Cambridge: Harvard University Press.

Appendices

Appendix 1:
A SUPPORTING DOCUMENT TO
INVESTIGATE THE NEED FOR DIFFERENTIATION

The document to investigate the need for differentiation is meant to be filled in together with the student, their parents and all adults who teach the student. One should remember that learning challenges do not manifest in similar ways at home and at school, or even in all school subjects. Thus, each party can fill in their own document, if needed. The classroom teacher or form teacher can then compile these documents together.

The more a student has 'yes' tick marks, the more systematically one should differentiate their learning. You can get tips for the objective of differentiation from the 'areas' column, and the column that is furthest right.

INVESTIGATION OF THE NEEDS FOR DIFFERENTIATION

Name and class: _____

Filled by: _____

Area	Yes	No	Subject or situation where exhibited
Social skills and behaviour			
Student often gets into conflicts that they cannot solve independently			
Student often disrupts teaching			
Student daydreams in class or does not pay attention to teaching			
Work skills			
Student cannot follow teacher's instructions			
Student cannot complete work during lesson			
Student does not sit still			
Student clearly works more slowly than classmates			
Student consistently finishes work more quickly than classmates			
Assessment			
Student does not reach goals, or reaches them barely			
Student runs out of time with tasks, or they get their work done clearly before others			
Student performs clearly worse or better than their age group			
Student consistently gets full marks on tests, or they do not have to ever struggle with their work			
Homework			
Student consistently spends unreasonable amounts of time on homework (30 mins for lower grade levels, 1 hour for higher grade levels)			
Student usually cannot complete homework independently			
Homework puts unreasonable burden on the student			
Homework is often left undone			
Student never has work left to do at home			

Appendix 2:
A BAG OF TRICKS FOR DIFFERENTIATION

We have compiled some practical tips for differentiation, based on this book, according to the 5D model of differentiation. The bag of tricks for differentiation does not attempt to be an exhaustive list of methods for differentiation. Instead, it is meant for the teacher as stimulation for the differentiation of their own teaching. In the document, only some methods are highlighted for each dimension of differentiation, and you can fill in the list yourself as you go. The bag of tricks can be used as a template, when the school as a whole considers appropriate methods for differentiation. Well-received and practical solutions should be shared within the school.

This document can be used, alongside pedagogical documents, for quick relay of information about the methods that have been tried in the classroom, for example after consulting a school psychologist regarding the students' learning.

It is advisable to write the working practices down in the student's pedagogical documents for further use.

THE BAG OF TRICKS FOR DIFFERENTIATION: TEACHING ARRANGEMENTS

Tick actions that have already been taken. If needed, add more:

- ☐ The student has taken part in remedial teaching, either alone or in a group.
- ☐ The student has taken part in proactive remedial teaching.
- ☐ The student has used a learning assistant for support.
- ☐ The student has taken part in special needs education, either alone or in a group.
- ☐ The student has received special needs education through co-teaching, along with the rest of the class.
- ☐ The student has taken part in another grade's (same, lower or higher) lesson.
- ☐ There have been multiple teachers present during the lesson (i.e. co-teaching).
- ☐ Flexible grouping has been utilised in the student's own classroom (based on skills, teaching content, work styles, social relationships or areas of interest).
- ☐ Flexible grouping has been tried within the grade level, or across grade levels.
- ☐ Split lessons have been used in teaching, with different groupings.
- ☐ Lessons have been paralleled with classes from the same or different grade level, in order to allow for flexible grouping.
- ☐ Teaching groups have occasionally been reduced in size through parallel lessons.
- ☐ The student's school day has been temporarily made shorter (check local legislation).

- ☐ _____
- ☐ _____
- ☐ _____

THE BAG OF TRICKS FOR DIFFERENTIATION: THE LEARNING ENVIRONMENT

Tick actions that have already been taken. If needed, add more:

THE PHYSICAL LEARNING ENVIRONMENT

☐ The student's seat has been placed far from distractions, such as doors or windows.

☐ Individual learning habits and needs have been discussed with the student and the whole class.

☐ The student's individual needs have been verbalised to the student, and the student has understood them.

☐ Physical requirements for learning have been checked in the classroom (e.g. air quality, temperature and lighting).

☐ The teacher has made sure the student can see the board.

☐ The workstation has been adjusted to fit the student.

☐ The workstation has been cornered off by screens.

☐ The workstation has been moved closer to the teacher.

☐ The student has been seated next to a student who pays attention well.

☐ Different seating arrangements have been tried in the classroom (in groups, in pairs or alone).

☐ The classroom has been kept tidy and organised (i.e. visuals on the walls are intact and straight).

☐ Everything has a labelled place in the classroom.

☐ Excess stimuli have been taken off the walls (e.g. pictures and posters).

☐ Different workstations have been organised in the classroom (e.g. group work, reading station).

☐ Different spaces in the school have been utilised for differentiation.

☐ Individual distractions have been minimised (e.g. by using headphones, hats and hoods).

☐ Concentration has been directed individually, for example through allowing listening to music.

☐ The student's individual work has been tested in different places in the classroom (e.g. sofa, the floor).

☐ Individual visual support materials have been tested with the student.

☐ _____

☐ _____

☐ _____

THE BAG OF TRICKS FOR DIFFERENTIATION: THE LEARNING ENVIRONMENT

Tick actions that have already been taken. If needed, add more:

THE PSYCHO-SOCIAL LEARNING ENVIRONMENT

☐ The class has been grouped together properly.

☐ The student's seating has been chosen so that it supports interaction and the student's personality.

☐ Individual break practices have been tested with the student (e.g. only going to certain places during the break, limited break time, breaks with an adult or indoor breaks).

☐ New situations and transitions have been pre-emptively gone through with the student.

☐ The student has had a permanent group, peer support partner or mentor, with whom they have worked.

☐ Teaching groups have been varied and they have been formed according to the teacher's instructions.

☐ Communication and interaction have been practiced in class.

☐ The student has used a differentiated way to answer questions in class.

☐ Differentiative working culture has been verbalised in class.

☐ Performance and presentation situations have been anticipated and differentiated in class.

☐ _____

☐ _____

☐ _____

THE BAG OF TRICKS FOR DIFFERENTIATION: TEACHING METHODS

Tick actions that have already been taken. If needed, add more:

☐ Study techniques have been practiced with the student (e.g. having the appropriate equipment, reading techniques, the correct steps to complete work, preparing for a test).

☐ Pictures or textual support have been used in class in addition to oral instructions.

☐ The student has received individual instructions for their work.

☐ The student has used action cards or action cards have been used in the classroom in general.

☐ The student has progressed individually with the content.

☐ The student has had individual performance goals in class (e.g. only answering with one word).

☐ Working time has been individualised for the student (e.g. using a time timer).

☐ Other students have been used to support the student's writing.

☐ The student has had the permission to answer and complete work orally, and record speech with a phone.

☐ The student has had differentiated homework (e.g. different number of exercises, different level of work or only work for certain content).

☐ The student has been supported with marking the homework and remembering it (e.g. homework notebook, support from teacher or peer).

☐ The student has completed homework orally or in pictures, and recorded this with a phone or tablet.

☐ The structure of the school day has been supported (e.g. clear beginnings and ends to lessons, keeping the daily schedule in view).

☐ The student has had an incentive system in place for successes.

☐ The student has received regular feedback for their successes.

☐ The student has used differentiated or individualised learning materials.

☐ The student has been set individual goals, and the student knows what they are.

☐ The student or the whole class has practised contractual project work.

☐ The class has tried station work.

☐ The class has tried project work.

☐ _____

☐ _____

☐ _____

THE BAG OF TRICKS FOR DIFFERENTIATION: SUPPORTING MATERIALS

Tick actions that have already been taken. If needed, add more:

☐ The student has used extra visual materials to support their learning (e.g. Multilink building blocks in mathematics).

☐ The student has used individualised textbooks or materials.

☐ The student has used materials from higher or lower grade levels.

☐ The student has used plain language texts.

☐ The student has used audiobooks to support their reading.

☐ The student has used a tablet or computer to support their reading.

☐ The student has not been expected to write by hand, and instead they have used a computer and a word-processing programme to support their reading.

☐ The student has used their own device in teaching (e.g. phone or tablet).

☐ The student has had special arrangements to direct their concentration (e.g. screens, headphones, hats or listening to music).

☐ The student has had special arrangements to direct physical energy during lessons (e.g. stress ball, balance board or moving in class).

☐ The student's work has been structured differently (e.g. hourglass, prescribed contractual project work).

☐ _____

☐ _____

☐ _____

THE BAG OF TRICKS FOR DIFFERENTIATION: ASSESSMENT

Tick actions that have already been taken. If needed, add more:

- ☐ The individual goals of the student have been set, and the student is aware of these.
- ☐ The student has taken part in setting their goals.
- ☐ The goals have been monitored regularly.
- ☐ The student has had a say in how their skills and learning is assessed.
- ☐ Self-assessment has been practiced and it has been done consistently, even during the completion of the work.
- ☐ A discussion on assessment has been consistently had with the student.
- ☐ Portfolios have been tested as a means of assessment.
- ☐ A learning journal has been tested as a means for assessment.
- ☐ Presentations have been tested as a means of assessment.
- ☐ Projects have been tested as a means of assessment.

- ☐ _____

- ☐ _____

- ☐ _____

TEST ARRANGEMENTS

Tick actions that have already been taken. If needed, add more:

☐ Preparation for a test has been differentiated by telling the student the test questions beforehand.

☐ The student has had a chance to come up with the test questions by themselves.

☐ The student has been tested orally.

☐ The student has had extra time on a test.

☐ The student has completed the test in parts.

☐ The student's understanding of the question has been ensured before answering it.

☐ The student has tried a take-home test.

☐ The student has had a completely differentiated test (e.g. multiple choice questions).

☐ _____

☐ _____

☐ _____

Appendix 3:
A SUPPORTING DOCUMENT FOR THE TEACHER

In differentiation, the student's progress can be monitored with a supporting document. It helps to keep in mind what has been tried already. The document can be filled in according to the five dimensions of differentiation, or by subject. The document can also work as a support for the pedagogical document. On the next few pages, there are examples of the use of this document. There is also an empty template on page 269, which can be used in your own teaching and its differentiation.

This document can be used to communicate the methods that have been tested in class when the student has begun to see a school psychologist and the student can be mentioned by name. Make sure you have the parents' permission for this.

The supporting document for the teacher is meant to support the teacher in their work. All working practices and important pedagogical observations should be written down in the student's pedagogical documents.

TEACHING ARRANGEMENTS

A SUPPORTING DOCUMENT FOR DIFFERENTIATION AND DRAFTING DOCUMENTS (Fill in as necessary)		
Name and class of the student: Amy 5A		
GENERAL TEACHING ARRANGEMENTS		
Action taken	When tried/confirmed?	Teacher's observations
Amy has taken part in remedial teaching.	Since 11.9.	Amy has shown up to remedial teaching.
Amy has taken part in proactive remedial teaching.	Since 1.10.	Since October, new content has been gone through with Amy in remedial teaching. This has clearly helped her with working in class. Pro-active remedial instruction has worked better than reactive.
Amy has had a learning assistant as support.	9.8.	Occasional lessons. The support of the assistant helps the whole class, not only Amy herself.
Amy has taken part in special education teaching either alone or in a group.	1.9.	
Amy has had special needs teaching as co-teaching, along with the rest of the class.	1.11	The SEN teacher has been present in mathematics lessons as a co-teacher.
Flexible grouping has been used in teaching.	9.8.	Humanities are often studied together with the other class in the same grade level, so Amy has been able to work at her level in a small group. Sometimes they have had a learning assistant to help them.
Group size has been reduced.	1.9.	Split lessons are not used, but the group size has been reduced with the help of the other grade 5 teacher in French. Amy studies French in a smaller group. The mathematics group is bigger, but there is a SEN teacher there to co-teach.

LEARNING ENVIRONMENT

A SUPPORTING DOCUMENT FOR DIFFERENTIATION AND DRAFTING DOCUMENTS (Fill in as necessary)		
Name and class of the student: Rasmus 3A		
THE LEARNING ENVIRONMENT		
Action taken	When tried/confirmed?	Teacher's observations
Rasmus' seat has been moved close to the teacher.	9.8. 30.8.	Added note 30.8. Did not significantly affect work during lesson.
Rasmus' seat has been cornered off by screens and it has been moved far from distractions.	30.8.	30.8. Rasmus' workstation has been moved to the edge of the class and it has been cornered off by screens. 5.9. Looks like it is working better.
Rasmus' individual needs have been verbalised to him and he has understood them.	30.8.	Rasmus' challenges are being verbalised actively out loud in the classroom. Rasmus collects stars for his successes, and regularly completes self-assessments at the end of each day.
Distractions have been strived to be limited individually.	30.8.	When working independently, Rasmus is allowed to listen to music. This helps him focus on his own work.
The class has been grouped together.	1.9.	Rasmus gets into conflicts during breaks often. During September, we will spend one language and literature lesson per week on group dynamics and practising communication. Added note 20.9. Rasmus has made friends in the class. Group work goes well with Thomas and Will.

TEACHING METHODS

A SUPPORTING DOCUMENT FOR DIFFERENTIATION AND DRAFTING DOCUMENTS (Fill in as necessary)		
Name and class of the student: Sam 1A		
TEACHING METHODS		
Action taken	When tried/confirmed?	Teacher's observations
Sam gets individual instructions for his work.	15.8.	Sam seems to need instructions to be confirmed to him individually.
Pictures used alongside verbal instructions. Daily schedule is put on the board in the morning.	15.8. 1.9.	The daily schedule is gone through in the mornings. The instructions for each class are written on the board. Added note 1.9. Sam has a hard time understanding the instructions on the board.
Sam has action cards, which are also used for the rest of the class.	1.9.	Action cards are kept at his desk.
Sam uses an incentive system for successes.	1.9.	Sam collects stamps in his notebook for each success. After a successful week, Sam has a reading or game lesson on Friday.
Sam gets differentiated homework. He marks his homework in a homework notebook.	1.9.	Sam's homework is mostly left undone. We'll try a homework notebook. Added note 15.10. Sam has finally understood how to use his homework notebook. A week without forgetting. We will continue as we have.
Sam has special arrangements in place to direct his physical energy.	1.9.	Sam uses a balance board. We have agreed on 'extra' pencil sharpening trips, so Sam gets to move in class.
Sam's work has been structured in different ways.	1.9. 15.10.	Sam can work for 5-10 minutes at a time. The work is split into parts so that Sam comes to the teacher to ask for the next exercise to complete. If work goes well, Sam can use an iPad to play a maths game for 15 minutes in the end of the lesson. 15.10. Consistent play of maths games has automatised adding up to 10. We will continue as we have.

SUPPORT MATERIALS

A SUPPORTING DOCUMENT FOR DIFFERENTIATION AND DRAFTING DOCUMENTS (Fill in as necessary)		
Name and class of the student: Amy 5A		
SUPPORT MATERIALS		
Action taken	When tried/confirmed?	Teacher's observations
Amy uses a lower grade level math book.	9.8.	Based on last year, a lower grade level book has been used.
Amy uses plain language texts	1.12. 12.1.	Amy has a hard time understanding long texts. Reading assignments should be kept short. Textbook summaries work well. In language and literature, plain language texts should be used. Added note 12.1. Amy has gotten into horses. Trying to build her work in French and language and literature based on this area of interest.
Amy uses a computer.	1.12.	Amy writes texts by computer and uses spell check to support spelling.

ASSESSMENT

A SUPPORTING DOCUMENT FOR DIFFERENTIATION AND DRAFTING DOCUMENTS (Fill in as necessary)		
Name and class of the student: Amy 5A		
ASSESSMENT		
Action taken	When tried/confirmed?	Teacher's observations
Amy's individual goals have been confirmed, and she knows them.	1.9.	Gone through with Amy and parents. Amy completes self-assessment every day.
Amy has had a say in how her learning is assessed (i.e. portfolio, learning journal, presentation)	1.10.	Amy gets nervous about tests. We will keep them to a minimum. We agreed that in science, she gets to show her skills through extra presentations. Amy can choose the topic herself.
Amy has special test arrangements (i.e. oral testing, take-home test, making sure she understands the questions)	1.10.	French test can be done orally. Vocabulary tests are not marked down for spelling if the word is recognisable.

MATHEMATICS

A SUPPORTING DOCUMENT FOR DIFFERENTIATION AND DRAFTING DOCUMENTS (Fill in as necessary)		
Name and class of the student: Catherine 9A		
MATHEMATICS		
Action taken	When tried/confirmed?	Teacher's observations
Catherine has an upper secondary school book to work on alongside the common materials.	15.9.	Catherine has worked on the book at the end of classes. Become a natural way to work.
Catherine has taken part in upper secondary school mathematics teaching.	1.10.	This arrangement helps Catherine, but is hard to make work (i.e. scheduling, progressing in teaching, transitioning). Will need to be worked on and better planned.
Catherine gets a test with more challenging questions.	1.11.	Test was successful. Will do this in the future.
Catherine has acted as a peer support occasionally towards the end of the lesson.	1.10.	Catherine has found peer supporting to be motivating, and it has helped the whole class.
Catherine has been assigned homework from the upper secondary book.	15.9.	The difficulty level seems appropriate. She has also been satisfied.

TEMPLATE

A SUPPORTING DOCUMENT FOR DIFFERENTIATION AND DRAFTING DOCUMENTS (Fill in as necessary)		
Name and class of the student:		
TOPIC/SUBJECT:		
Action taken	When tried/confirmed?	Teacher's observations

Appendix 4:
A TEMPLATE FOR SELF-ASSESSMENT

Self-assessment should be age-appropriate. Different leaflets or documents make progress visible, and work well as a basis for discussions. They also help the home to follow the student's progress. It is good to remember that although electronic tools work, information on paper sometimes travels best between the school and home.

Self-assessment should be completed and practised consistently. Depending on the topic, the object of assessment can be a lesson or a whole day. Goals need to be set so that they can be realistically achieved by the student. In the appendix, there are a pre-filled example, and an empty template.

SELF-ASSESSMENT

NAME AND CLASS:
Rasmus 3A

MY GOALS (SET TOGETHER WITH A TEACHER):
I won't hit others or call them names.

HOW I WILL SOLVE THIS:
If there's an argument during break, I will leave the situation. I'll find a break monitor. I'll resolve the problem with the teacher after the break.

MY ASSESSMENT AFTER EVERY LESSON:

	Success!	I didn't succeed	Comments
1st Lesson		x	Will annoyed me.
2nd Lesson		x	
3rd Lesson	x		
4th Lesson	x		
5th Lesson	x		
6th Lesson		x	

TEACHER'S FEEDBACK:
You were unreasonably harsh on yourself during the music lesson. You cannot always avoid conflicts. The most important thing is how you act during a conflict. Morning lessons went well as well. However, I do agree with you on the PE lesson in the afternoon. But you took part in resolving the situation and knew how to apologise.

A MESSAGE FROM HOME:
Overall, it looks like it went well. Rasmus came home feeling quite cheerful.

SELF-ASSESSMENT: TEMPLATE

NAME AND CLASS:

_____

MY GOALS (SET TOGETHER WITH A TEACHER):

_____

_____

HOW I WILL SOLVE THIS:

_____

_____

_____

MY ASSESSMENT AFTER EVERY LESSON:

	Success!	I didn't succeed	Comments
1st Lesson			
2nd Lesson			
3rd Lesson			
4th Lesson			
5th Lesson			
6th Lesson			

TEACHER'S FEEDBACK:

_____

_____

_____

A MESSAGE FROM HOME:

_____

_____

Appendix 5:
CARDS FOR WORKING AND TO DIRECT ACTION

In Appendix 5, we have compiled cards to support work and actions in class. You are free to photocopy these.

At the end of the appendix, there are empty card templates you can use to make your own cards. As we mentioned in Chapter 5, cards can be made with the students, the work can also be given to older students. Sometimes, a photo works better than a drawn picture. For example, one can take a picture of the textbook you use for a certain subject. In photos, the student can be a model for the appropriate action. That way, making the action cards can have a pedagogical meaning, and it is easier to tell the student what the appropriate actions and ways of working are.

Independent work

Pair or group work

Silence

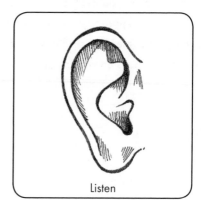

Listen

I won't hit

I won't curse

Free play or time

Break

Lunch

Music

PE

Crafts

Art

Put your hand up

Read

Check your work

Complete an exercise